ADVA
PRAISE

"Sandra has written a must-read primer for anyone considering a career in PR – and a valuable resource guide for anyone in communications period. I pulled out at least a dozen examples I plan to bring into the office with me on Monday to educate, reinforce and reenergize my own staff. Read this book and learn from one of the best."
Susan Flinn Cobian, President, HYC Health

"Sandra is someone who knows PR inside in out, from both a strategic standpoint as well as how to make great PR happen. *The Art & Craft of PR* is not only a great introduction to PR for those new to the discipline, it also has plenty of a-ha's and insights for the seasoned pro. I recommend it wholeheartedly."
Chip Walker, Director of Brand Strategy, Bloomberg Media

Published by
LID Publishing Limited
The Record Hall, Studio 204,
16-16a Baldwins Gardens,
London EC1N 7RJ, UK

524 Broadway, 11th Floor, Suite 08-120,
New York, NY 10012, US

info@lidpublishing.com
www.lidpublishing.com

A member of:

www.businesspublishersroundtable.com

Printed in Great Britain by TJ International
ISBN: 978-0-9991871-0-4

Cover and page design: Caroline Li & Matthew Renaudin

SANDRA STAHL

The Art & Craft of PR

Creating the mindset and skills to succeed in public relations today

LID

LONDON   NEW YORK   SHANGHAI
MADRID   BARCELONA   BOGOTA
MEXICO CITY   MONTERREY   BUENOS AIRES

CONTENTS

For Rae and Irwin Stahl

PROLOGUE

My parents never knew exactly what I did for a living. Sure, they would proudly tell people their daughter was in PR, and say things like, "You know, she always liked to talk." My father never stopped saying I was a "people person". My mother unceasingly asked why my name wasn't in the articles when I showed her a *New York Times* story I had just scored for a client or an *Associated Press* feature I had pitched.

Later, when I started to focus on healthcare, I'd tell my mother about the campaigns we put together for this company or that therapeutic area, and she would shake her head sadly and say in a disappointed and kind of horrified voice that my work was probably making people think they were sick.

I'd persist. I would explain that our screening programmes, for example, often helped bring critical health services to people who may not have access to regular care. And our efforts identified those at risk just as often as they informed others that they were *not* sick.

At the end of these conversations, my mother would invariably, grudgingly nod and say, "Alright, maybe you helped a few people, but that doesn't sound like PR. So, what did you say it was that you did?"

What *is* and what is *not* Public Relations is still under discussion, even among the most seasoned executives of our discipline. Where PR begins and ends, and the point at which PR evolves into something else, has been dissected in infinitesimal detail.

"I think we get too caught up in the nomenclature," said Dave Samson, General Manager of Public Affairs at Chevron, in one of several conversations we had. "It's a distraction. I just look at it as one large communications ecosystem."

Considering PR a part of communications is certainly one popular point of view, though others say that communications is a subset of PR; that communications is just a tool in the comprehensive PR toolbox we use to connect with stakeholders.

Whichever camp you are in, one thing on which nearly all agree is that it is the holistic definition of PR – not just one part of it or another – that ultimately matters. And that's because PR has a different endgame: the creation of meaningful relationships that contribute to the achievement of larger goals.

Indeed, the unique ability of PR to foster relationships – and not just any relationships, but trusted relationships – is what differentiates our discipline. PR has the capacity to build, support and, when called for, to leverage relationships.

It is this meaningful connection and not the tactics or channels used to get us there (whether these be press releases, video, social posts, tweets or special events, for example) that truly defines PR and has earned its place of value in the business world.

Our ability to articulate a position, establish what a company or brand stands for, and determine its values and goals is part of that process. Add to that the reading and understanding of a situation, the insight underpinning the foundation and scale of the relationship. This is what I'd call the art of PR. Mastery of the fundamentals, and the tools and channels we use to bring that articulation and the relationship to life, is its finely honed craft.

These days, however, the art can easily get lost in the craft. Social, digital, content, mobile... these are hot buttons, all too often mistakenly considered the 'keys' to PR today and, more importantly, its ability to grow and continue to be important to business.

I asked Paul Holmes, Chair of The Holmes Group, who has been writing about public relations for more than 25 years, if he felt the balance of the art and the craft was teetering out of whack.

"Implementation may well be overwhelming the strategy level," Holmes said. "Most people, including what I'd suggest are the vast majority of practitioners today, have gotten the relationship between the discipline and the practice entirely wrong."

He continued, "Most PR professionals are part counsellor, part implementer. And there will always be those who are stronger at one than the other. But we must give every aspiring practitioner and emerging leader in our industry the chance to develop both sides. We have to avoid an emphasis on craftsmanship, if only in the hope that craftsmen will eventually become counsellors, that they'll develop the empathy and the thinking over time. We have to underscore the importance of both roles from the start."

Charlotte Otto, former Global External Relations Officer at Procter & Gamble, felt similarly when I spoke with her.

"It seems social media has gotten us all confused – it's a tactic, but people think oh, that's PR because it offers accessible communication and the immediate potential for engagement. This misunderstanding has led us down the wrong path. PR has always been about relationship building and influence using multi-platform communications and engagement. Social media just allows us to do this in real-time. You know, there was a great debate, when broadcast advertising budgets started to balloon, that PR was going to have to adjust or it would suffer as a discipline. It's the same now. We can't get so absorbed in the tactics that we lose the big picture."

I agree.

Personally, I always get excited about what's new in the PR toolbox, and have been an early adopter of vehicles that give us greater amplification and reach with better speed.

These new options are fun to use, effective, and highly cost-efficient. Indeed, PR folks were among the first to embrace social media because we saw the incredible potential for connecting with our audiences. It naturally fell into our realm. We embraced the original 140-character limit of Twitter with our skills at writing concise messages and created Facebook communities through storytelling. We integrate traditional media across social platforms seamlessly.

But I never forget that many of these very same tools and channels are available to others outside of PR, who self-identify as, among other titles, content specialists, content marketers, or influencer strategists.

What makes PR professionals so valuable is our ability to use the evolving channels, tactics and resources in service of a greater objective of developing relationships that matter. Relationships that solve business needs, address critical issues and create communities.

With strong skills in both the art and the craft, PR professionals can support the internal stakeholders in the C-suite, public affairs, government affairs, employees, sales, public policy and marketing executives as well as external stakeholders. With both sets of the PR equation firmly in place, we are adept at reading the spoken and behavioural cues of a target audience, building meaningful and enduring relationships, and articulating the message, culture or philosophy of the organization, brand or company we're representing.

This book is built around the idea that PR is and has always been distinct. Our future is not confined to our ability to own the latest tools available or make the most unique or innovative use of them. We don't have a 'swim lane' or a 'silo' that confines our professional capabilities or growth.

Throughout these pages, readers will find a user's manual for developing and nurturing the mindset required for the art of PR together with the fundamental skillset necessary for executing the craft. It is not necessary to practice all of the recommendations to enhance success. Rather, I hope to have presented a portfolio of strategies and insights that will inspire PR practitioners of today and tomorrow.

CHAPTER 1

PR
HAS NO
BOUNDARIES

"*If you define PR for businesses as the art and science of engaging people at scale to believe something and then act upon that, then there are no boundaries to what we can do in our industry. It's age old. It's only the channels we use that come and go rapidly.*"

Jon Iwata, former Senior Vice President, Chief Brand Officer, IBM

Many years ago, my jacobstahl partner, Jeremy, worked for View-Master®, maker of the classic toy that brought the world to kids through special plastic scopes and cardboard circles of colour transparencies. The client, Elliot, was about the same age as Jeremy and a marketing maverick of his time.

One day, Elliot came to the office to discuss the launch of a cool, cutting-edge View Master offering. Like the new product, the marketing communications needed to go beyond the expected. He immediately turned to PR for the solution and, as inspiration, told Jeremy to go back to his "rock and roll roots" to develop a plan that, in today's vernacular, would be described as 'disruptive'.

He expected PR to meet this challenge with something new and different that would surprise and delight the target audience and inspire behavioural change.

That Elliot turned to PR is not surprising. Our industry has both the excellent fundamentals (more on those in the next chapter) and the imaginative 'chops' to tackle an ever-widening array of challenges and serve as the primary communications catalyst for any brand challenge. PR has long been a valuable part of a marketing mix, but it can also lead change and forge new pathways.

Whenever I've had clients like Elliot and the opportunity to step outside the traditional or even the so-called 'modern' (now 'standard') digital and social tactics, I am reminded of how deeply it is possible to mine our discipline for *all* kinds of communications answers.

There is an abundance of creative, instructive and very effective PR that deserves reward and admiration. Reading case studies and talking to seasoned professionals about what proved effective and what didn't can offer limitless lessons. There are many excellent sources worth checking out: industry online and print publications like *The Holmes Report* and *PRWeek*, the Public Relations Society of America website, books written by industry executives and even PR agency websites, which showcase excellent case studies.

Luckily, there is plenty of room within PR to stretch. We're not even close to hitting the ceiling of our communications capabilities. That's what I tell our jacobstahl team, as well as my students in the Brand and Integrated Communications master's degree programme at City College of new York, where I am an adjunct professor. Our skills as strategists, storytellers, and purveyors of influence can and should take PR in an infinite number of directions – if we allow them to, if the communications challenge we're working on demands it, and if we find the opportunities.

After all, we PR practitioners are master developers of compelling narratives. We have deep and abiding respect for the power of language, individual words, sounds, looks and feeling. There is no reason our role in narrating a brand or company story to stakeholders can't begin far earlier in the process with the creative development of the brand's phonetics and optics. We have tactics and channels at our disposal but, far more importantly, we have a broader perspective drawn from our industry's rich history, that can prove truly influential and transformative in creating a story about a particular brand.

Austrian-American Edward James Bernays, who died in 1995 after an eventful life spanning 103 years, is recognized as the 'father' of PR. The nephew of Sigmund Freud, he pioneered many techniques for influencing public opinion, which he called the "engineering of consent."[1] In today's vernacular, I suppose that would form the equivalent of 'getting to a yes'.

Bernays never lost sight of the business value of PR: "Public relations, effectively used, helps validate an underlying principle of our society – competition in the market place of ideas and things," he wrote in 1971.

Tactically, Bernays went far beyond media relations, or 'press agentry', though he had great success generating publicity for his clients. Besides earned media, he used endorsements from opinion leaders, celebrities, doctors, and other experts as part of his campaigns – a technique we'd refer to these days as an 'influencer strategy'.

He employed many other PR tools still in use: consistent messaging, public opinion polls, events and word of mouth. One of my favourite campaigns he orchestrated was for Ivory soap. The objective: making bathing more popular with children. The solution: a national panel of small-sculpture experts that oversaw soap carving competitions, to significant and enduring acclaim.

If we were executing the Ivory campaign today, we'd likely enlist the support of Mom bloggers, post videos of the competitions and encourage participation that would be shared on social media.

The founders of some of the largest global PR agencies always viewed their discipline through a wide lens; from the earliest days, their solutions for clients were multi-dimensional and used multiple platforms. When David Finn and Bill Ruder started their agency Ruder Finn in 1948 they never thought of themselves as 'media' people, explains Franklin Walton, Ph.D., member of the Measurement Commission at the Institute for PR and long-time guru. "That early generation drew on whatever communications they needed – lobbying, advertising, influencer communications, media outreach, events, everything."[2]

The early giants of our field brought deep and developed skills to the practice that reflected politics and pop culture, and drew on history, psychology and philosophy to develop their successful programming. Good models then and now. An excellent source for history is The Museum of Public Relations in New York City.[3]

Mike Fernandez drew on our industry background when he spoke to me from the global agency Burson-Marsteller where he is Chief Executive Officer.

"Harold Burson and Bill Marsteller created the firm in 1953. It was essentially the joining of two distinct organizations: Bill brought his advertising and marketing firm together with Harold's PR agency. So, while the idea of 'integrated communications' has been talked about over the last 10 or 15 years as a new idea, in fact that's what Burson-Marsteller offered back in the 1950s. And everyone who worked there from that time had this full-circle perspective. Public relations and integrated communications were seen as vital. This is not necessarily the normal experience today for a lot of people just entering the PR industry. Many people tend to get boxed in; they use a specific communications tactic using specific tools, rather than respond to a request to solve a problem. So, we end up being focused on tactics rather than strategy. I encourage our teams here and our clients to look at needs and opportunities holistically – not to just come up with communication or an ad. Public relations is about relating to the public in ways that solve problems. That's the historical intent of this profession and will, ironically, allow us to capture the future."

Like Fernandez, I believe the roots of our business are both instructive and inspiring, and I encourage learning about the industry's founders and earliest work. But I also believe it's crucial to foster a little restlessness. Sometimes I tell young colleagues and students that 'no' is just the first two letters of 'not yet'.

We must regularly challenge ourselves as well as our peers, colleagues and clients to think more broadly, more strategically, and not just default to the path of least resistance. It can be up to the PR practitioner in a roomful of people, gathered to create a strategy or manage a thorny business issue, to say that changing the message or throwing a tactic at a problem is not going to work; that the only solution that will be effective is one that is more complex, has more steps and requires more effort – sometimes even wholesale change.

"The advice that is given by good PR counsellors often involves a lot of hard work – a good PR counsellor will look at a problem and, if necessary, say to a company leader that they need to change their organizational behaviour, corporate policies, decision making, even the culture of the company, if that is what it will take to have a positive relationship with the company's stakeholders," explains Holmes.

Look no further than British Petroleum – an example Holmes likes to use to illustrate his point. In 2000, the company decided to broaden its business to include a focus on renewable energy. 'Beyond Petroleum' was its $200 million advertising and public relations answer.[4] A comprehensive effort, the campaign included a new logo, advertising, paid and earned media and more. The disconnect, however, was that everything inside the company remained essentially as it had always been. Nothing else about the company's behaviour changed. This rendered the campaign and the messaging empty and inauthentic, and, by 2013, BP had quietly gone back to basics.

The takeaway: it is always easier to change the communications than the business or a company's behaviour. It takes a considered, evidence-based strategic argument put forward by a thoughtful and artful PR counsellor to make the case that a campaign alone, no matter how creative or comprehensive, is only a campaign. Effective communications need serious thought and true reflection. There is a need for challenging and sometimes difficult discussions to go far deeper into the potential solutions. Such an approach requires strategic PR professionals, who are equipped to lead a company down the harder road.

"PR is not about promoting one thing or another. It's being clear with all our stakeholders."

Margery Kraus, Founder and Executive Chairman, APCO Worldwide

The desire to go beyond the easy solution – to take a risk, to use new channels if they are appropriate and in service to the overarching goal – pushes us past our own boundaries and will help drive the kind of focused, and occasionally freewheeling, curiosity and exploration that make PR invaluable.

"Sometimes the industry is so worried about competition from other disciplines, it loses sight of the strategic value it can add by just coming up with good and bold ideas that don't pay attention to boundaries," offers Margery Kraus, Founder and Executive Chairman of APCO.

Embracing the freedoms inherent in our discipline will allow us to restate the value of our profession at a time when many of the issues companies face occur because of a failure to engage with the right stakeholders at the right time, and transpire because of misjudgement or the misreading of various stakeholder groups and what's important to them.

James Grunig and Todd Hunt published a book called *Managing Public Relations* in 1984.[5] Considered seminal in its time, the authors describe two models of PR: two-way asymmetric and two-way symmetric approaches.[6]

Michael Turney describes these the following way:[7]

TWO-WAY ASYMMETRIC PUBLIC RELATIONS:

· Employs social science methods to develop more persuasive communication;

· Generally focuses on achieving short-term attitude change;

· Incorporates substantial feedback from target audiences and public sectors;

· Is used by an organization primarily interested in having the public come around to its way of thinking, rather than changing the organization, its policies, or its views.

TWO-WAY SYMMETRIC PUBLIC RELATIONS:

· Relies on honest and open two-way communication and mutual give-and-take rather than one-way persuasion;

· Focuses on mutual respect and efforts to achieve mutual understanding;

- Emphasizes negotiation and a willingness to adapt and make compromises;

- Requires organizations engaging in public relations to be willing to make significant adjustments in how they operate in order to accommodate their public;

- Seems to be used by non-profit organizations, government agencies, and heavily regulated businesses such as public utilities, more than by competitive, profit-driven companies.

Simply put, the two-way asymmetrical model uses persuasion and manipulation to encourage people to think a certain way and allows for a give and take, but with one party advancing a single point of view. Two-way symmetric PR takes a more problem-solving approach and strives to yield mutual understanding.

These are models that have since been re-examined and debated for their relevance today. What do you think? My view is that models lend structure to a practice but should not be considered as setting rigid boundaries that must be followed to the letter. For effective and boundary-less PR in today's communications environment, practitioners should first place themselves in the shoes of their stakeholders. And then, from that vantage point, they should consider their impact on the business or organization, rather than the other way around, and let insights derived from that understanding drive their strategy and tactics.

CHAPTER 2

THE

PR

FUNDAMENTALS

*"Inspiration is for amateurs.
The rest of us just show up
and get to work."*

Chuck Close[8]

There is no substitute for a healthy and steadfast dedication to the fundamentals. I have always believed carefully honed basics provide the confidence that sets us free creatively and intellectually, incentivize us to keep refining our skill sets, and – for a long and fruitful career – ensure we never get bored.

My devotion to fundamentals is hardly unique. This is why I'm always so surprised to hear Human Resources heads and recruiters say they have noticed a drop off – some describe it as significant – in what they call a "dedication to the fundamentals" among new applicants for PR roles.

Bill Straub, coach of the famed women's bowling team at the University of Nebraska, is well known for his rigorous emphasis on fundamentals. He believes mastery of these skills is the only way to reach one's full potential. In fact, his recruitment strategy is not to tell the super talented girls how awesome they are and how they'll contribute to a winning team, but to instead entice them with a promise that he will make them better if they allow him. Coach Straub's fundamentals drills are so intense, his critics refer to it as "clonehusking", a term that could sound derogatory but apparently doesn't disturb his winning team or Straub.[9]

Mastery of PR fundamentals is no different. And it is important to realize from the start that you'll likely achieve *mastery* with a lower case 'm' relatively quickly, but that you'll practice and perfect and evolve these same skills throughout your life to get to *Mastery*. It is work; you'll need to be relentless.

A great deal of PR programming, from brand support to crisis management, is based on these core elements: strategic planning, audience segmentation, message development, a central idea, channel selection and management and spokesperson preparation.

Contained within these elements are steps that need to be taken with care and precision. These are the fundamentals.

Ask any seasoned PR practitioner what their top list of fundamentals is and you'll likely get some overlap and some differences. Here is my top 10 list of absolute must-have core PR fundamentals:

1. CURIOSITY

Albert Einstein once said, "Once you stop learning, you start dying."[10] Learning takes place everywhere if you're present and open to it. There is no right way to do it. An active investment in learning doesn't need to be formal, though all types of classes and one-day programmes are widely available in-person and online. Informal, everyday opportunities abound. This may include reading, exploring new neighbourhoods and geographies even within your own city. Simply talking to people and asking questions can be eye-opening and professionally valuable. Learning can also take place as a quiet activity. Daydreaming, meditation and silent observation all work. The actor Vince Vaughn, in conversation with author Tim Ferris at the Vulture Festival in New York City, put it best when he said, "Learn how to learn. Learn how you learn. There's more than one way to the waterfall."

2. MESSAGE AND MOTIVE INTEGRITY

For too long, PR has been associated with 'spin', a term that I always felt was derisive. PR is not employed to make a negative sound like a positive. If a negative is really a negative, then the best PR advice is to face it, own it with care and respect, learn from it, address it, and then put it behind you and move on. With good planning and some luck, you may succeed in turning a negative into a positive in time. Trust is among the most important attributes we have as human beings and is a crucial element leaders of companies and organizations must possess as makers of brands they sell and representatives of a cause. Trust should always drive messaging, materials and channel-agnostic activations. Integrity is at the core of trust and truly remains the only way to be credible. As golfers would say, you don't get many mulligans here. In other words, there are very few opportunities for do-overs once trust is compromised.

3. EMPATHY

Awareness about the sensibilities, the opinions and the perspectives of others is the underpinning of successful PR. In its purest form, empathy puts you in touch with your target audience in a way that is almost intimate. It's an extremely useful power to have in any form of communication. Scratching the surface of empathy is never enough. To be empathetic to your stakeholders, you need to study their habits and their daily activities through research – via the means of quantitative data either utilizing a questionnaire of your own design or existing data. Supplement that with information gleaned from sources including blogs, message boards and articles from reliable sources and in-person interviews, if possible. Above all, take care not to view the findings of your research or the preferences, feelings or actions of a target audience through the prism of your own experiences or your own preferences.

"In the age of selfies, it takes discipline to take yourself out of the messaging, what appeals to you, as you do your homework," said Kathryn Beiser, Chief Communications Officer and Senior Vice President at Kaiser Permanente.

4. AGILITY

There is a reason many new or self-described 'boutique' PR agencies describe themselves as 'nimble'. These are typically smaller, flatter organizations with fewer people and simpler processes. The *need* to move quickly – either proactively or responsively – has always been critical to effective communications. However, due to the increasing number of channels and the 24/7 nature of news and content, the *ability to* move quickly has driven larger agencies, organizations and corporate PR departments to improve and many are now better at this than ever. Agility can be demonstrated in many ways. Understanding the communications preferences of your current and desired stakeholders will help channel your agility-readiness. For example: does your audience like lots of detail in their communications, or short, digestible bites? Which channels are they using and watching most? What and whom do they find most credible? Whether in rapid communications or the kind you can plan, you always need to be able to motivate your audience to sit up, listen, engage, participate or take action. More on this in Chapter 8.

5. WRITING CRISP, CLEAN, COMPLETE SENTENCES

As the Founder of *The Holmes Report*, a leading PR industry publication, Paul Holmes is in regular touch with people from all over the PR industry, corporate and agency executives from the C-suite to Human Resources and recruiters. He says the biggest complaint he gets from those who hire PR people is about writing skills they feel are sub-optimal (he used a stronger word).

It is not as if writing a pithy 140-character tweet is not a valuable skill. It is. Who would have predicted this could get one into the top job at The White House? But the ability to deliver a solid, engaging, seemingly old-fashioned complete sentence is non-negotiable. Proper prose matters.

Mary Lynn Carver, Chief Communications Officer and Global Vice President at General Mills, cites clarity of writing as the key to PR and, indeed, to all communications. She says, "Can you succinctly and clearly articulate complex ideas? Can you boil them down and make them simple? Can you sit in a meeting or cover an event and quickly deliver in writing the essence of what your audience needs? This has to be second nature to a PR person. It also contributes to effective visual storytelling. In putting together pictures, videos, animation, even infographics, people should not lose that it all starts with a clear articulation of your messages, a turn of phrase, something memorable that can be restated."

Articulated simply, if you can write clear sentences, it follows that you can think them and you can speak them and you will be a more confident and effective communicator as a result.

A virtually guaranteed way to strengthen one's writing is to practice, practice, practice. And read.

6. AN ABILITY TO WORK TOGETHER

Working as a team makes everyone – and therefore your combined output – stronger. There are many aspects to developing this ability. I will highlight just three:

Identify your own strengths

Dr. Martin Seligman, Director of the Positive Psychology Center at the Penn Master of Applied Positive Psychology programme, suggests a series of exercises to help people identify their signature strength. Among these is to write down an anecdote about a time when you were at your best. It doesn't need to be a life-changing event, but should have a clear beginning, middle and end. Re-read it every day for a week and each time, ask yourself, "What strengths did I display when I was at my best?" Note your answers. Did you show creativity? Good judgment? Were you supportive to others? Writing down your answers puts you in touch with what you're good at. The next step is to contemplate how to use these strengths to your advantage, intentionally organizing and structuring your life around them.[11]

Collaborate

Deloitte's Future of Work research found 65% of the C-Level executives surveyed have a strategic objective to transform their organization's culture with a focus on connectivity, communication, and collaboration.[12] The ability to collaborate – to reach across functions, to work cross-functionally, to get out of one's silos, whatever you want to call it – is the holy grail of every work environment. It is absolutely possible, and sometimes most efficient, to use technology such as shared drives, group emails and texts, and services like Skype, to collaborate. But I also believe the occasional human contact makes a difference, even if it's just via telephone. There is no substitute for a handshake, eye contact, recognizing the change in tone when people talk, and the ability to read the body language of others in developing a collaborative relationship.

Be helpable

Take and give constructive support. Sometimes this feels like, and is indeed, criticism. Remembering that feedback makes you and your work stronger can soften the sting, whether you are on the giving or receiving end.

7. UNDERSTAND DATA AND DATA ANALYTICS

PR practitioners will always need to be able to read, understand and interpret data and use advanced analytics in their core capabilities.

Dave Samson, General Manager of Public Affairs at Chevron, is in the natural resource business. He considers data to be PR's natural resource. "We now have access to incredible amounts of data. It's a game-changer. Data gives you the information you need to predict your target audiences' preferences and behaviour reliably, based on their past actions. We couldn't do that before. We used to rely on public opinion polls, their attitudes, but that doesn't necessarily mean they would do as we predicted," he explains.

He gave me a hypothetical example of the value of data in his world. One of Chevron's aims is to understand their stakeholders' perspectives on environmental causes. So, they conduct surveys, asking people how committed they are to the environment. The answer from most is "very", which shows that the environment and environmental conservation is important to them. The data analytics tell a different story. Data from the same group shows that most have never supported environmental causes, either through volunteer work or financially. Most have two Hummers or a similar type of car in their driveway. The majority don't make plans with concerns for their carbon footprint. It's clear that their everyday practices do not match their intentions. Understanding this allows Chevron to predict with greater certainty what their behaviour may be in response to communications or programming they develop.

There is a plethora of tools available to capture data sets that are directly actionable for PR. Practitioners can, for example, conduct sentiment analysis, long considered a go-to social listening metric to determine how target consumers feel about a particular brand. Tools are also available to drill down further for emotion measurement. These can be most helpful when the goal is to capture the hearts of your stakeholders, to help them connect emotionally to your message and encourage them to share some of themselves as part of the call-to-action. Lists of tools – some available free of charge, and others available for purchase – can easily be found online. Using data, PR professionals can test their ideas and the selected channels they use. Similarly, data provides the answer to the question about whether an activity should be scaled up or down. These predictive analytics and algorithms add certainty.

"I will reinforce that, in addition to possessing strong and varied communications skills, practitioners in the future will need to be able to process data and use advanced analytics in their core capabilities, along with a strong sense of how to apply behavioural science into their engagement practices."

Dave Samson, General Manager of Public Affairs, Chevron

8. STORY TELLING

Jon Iwata, former Senior Vice President and Chief Brand Officer at IBM, dislikes it when PR professionals are described as storytellers. "I am not a fan," he says, pointing out that storytelling is really just another (albeit important) tactic in our expanding portfolio.

I agree. Besides, the idea of 'storytelling' and being a 'storyteller' is already so hackneyed. It is used as a selling point by every type of communicator in every channel. Too often, the term is also used incorrectly.

That said, as a tactic, Iwata agrees storytelling has a place. "The most effective stories involve the human experience and how, in some way, we manage the unexpected."

"People tend to refer to PR as storytelling, and, yes, storytelling is part of it. But fundamentally our business is built on understanding human behaviour and what drives humans and groups of humans to change their behaviour. It's akin to cultural anthropology – ferreting out what it takes to influence groups of people to feel a certain way or take a certain action. It also takes understanding why stakeholders think what they think about your company or organization."

Mary Lynn Carver, Chief Communications Officer and Global Vice President, General Mills

When developing company or brand stories as part of our PR programming, I often look to authors I admire for inspiration. Anton Chekhov is a top choice for many reasons, but chiefly because he developed six principles that "make for a good story".[13] If they were good enough for this influential literary figure, they are certainly good enough for me! Here they are:

1. Absence of lengthy verbiage

2. Total objectivity

3. Truthful descriptions

4. Extreme brevity

5. Audacity and originality ("flee the stereotype")

6. Compassion

For more information about these principles, or if you would like to read about Chekov, it is worthwhile finding *The Letters of Anton Chekhov* online.

9. MEASUREMENT

If I had a nickel, or even a penny, for every discussion I've had, or every article I've read, about how to measure PR, I'd be rich. Oh, the handwringing that has gone into the return on investment (ROI) for PR versus, say, paid advertising on any channel – whether it be mobile, social, print, outdoor or broadcast, all of which are associated with a 'hard' return.

While both disciplines are responsible for creating relationships of a sort, advertising is based on creating a revenue-producing relationship with stakeholders. PR can certainly achieve this, but it is not its sole or even its primary purpose.

Charlotte Otto, former Global External Relations Officer at Procter & Gamble, said, "For marketing communications, we need to demonstrate an ROI relative to the marketing mix. It can be done and it's a cop-out that PR shouldn't or can't achieve this. However, on the corporate side, it's much more difficult to tie PR to ROI. There, we're looking for different outcomes that are more difficult to measure: improved reputation, a boost in visibility among the right audiences, awareness of our messages and other very specific metrics that can be attributed to developing and protecting our relationships."

Relationship-building can be difficult, though not impossible, to link to sales. Because of this perception, some business leaders and marketing executives pigeonhole PR as a 'nice to have' but not a 'must have'. I can think of three occasions right off the top of my head when I lost 90% of my PR budget to direct-to-consumer (DTC) advertising. I'll never forget when a client with whom we had a particularly strong relationship cut our hard-won budget to a fraction. That he delivered this news on my birthday made this that much more memorable! He was very apologetic, of course, but explained that he was persuaded to run a national broadcast ad campaign instead to generate a short-term sales boost and shifted our budget accordingly.

If I were working for IBM, it is unlikely PR would have lost its funding, or at least not for that reason.

"The R in PR doesn't stand for revenue," said Jon Iwata. "PR and communications should not be exclusively synonymous with sales and revenue. It can sometimes take an enlightened leader, whether on the marketing end or in the C-suite, to realize that."

The ability to measure our value to a business or a brand has been enhanced by data. There are a variety of services we can employ now that enable PR to test, validate and then measure the effectiveness of our messaging and the activities we implement. For comprehensive campaigns, such as a product launch, is still best to apply the appropriate measures to every element of an integrated effort – as it is the collective performance that will drive the outcome.

"If your company wants a relationship with its stakeholders, it's all about communications. What's the message? Will they find it compelling? How will it resonate best? And then the company needs to be consistent, communicate with integrity, and build trust. This is how PR helps a business move forward."

Emily Denney,
Vice President, Global Communications and Corporate Philanthropy, West Pharmaceutical Services

Finally, and this last point should not be underestimated, measurement of results should never be confused with accountability. PR should *always* be accountable and, in that respect, is no different from any other function within an organization.

10. ON BEING AN 'EXPERT'

You have expertise, of course, but to present yourself as an expert in any professional situation suggests you have nothing else to learn. As Carol Dweck, Lewis and Virginia Eaton Professor of Psychology at Stanford University and the author of *Mindset* says, "Why waste time proving over and over how great you are when you could be getting better?"[14] Dweck uses a simple metaphor of a 'know-it-all' vs. a 'learn-it-all' to make her point. Microsoft Chief Executive Officer Satya Nadella cites this metaphor as an inspiration for his business culture.

In her book, Dweck describes two kids at school, a know-it-all and a learn-it-all. The learn-it-all will always do better than the other student, even if the know-it-all starts with more innate capability.

Many persuasive reasons exist for staying a novice. For one thing, it prevents complacency. And another, it keeps you hungry. I'll leave you with my favourite reason from the screenwriter, William Goldman who famously said, "Nobody knows anything."

CHAPTER 3

THINK ATTRACTION, NOT PROMOTION

"If you change the way you look at things, the things you look at change."

Wayne Dyer[15]

Here's a million dollar question about PR and promotion: If we are making connections and changing minds, doesn't this require a *two-way* relationship?

Therein lies a critical insight, one that frequently, and oddly, is often hidden – the difference between promotion and attraction.

Promotion is one-way communication, a 'push' of information via any one or collection of channels. It is, essentially, a demand to be heard and seen. From the perspective of the target audience, it is a receipt of information, wanted or unwanted.

Viewed positively, promotion can inspire curiosity. It creates awareness. It makes an offer. Promotion can also provoke an action, whether this is information-seeking or something more.

Conversely, promotion asks for stakeholder time, attention and consideration, without regard to their schedule or need. As a result, promotion can be perceived as irritating. Invasive. Unsolicited. Something to be ignored.

Attraction is different. Attraction is mutual. It is a joint desire to connect. The receipt of information, in the case of attraction, is usually wanted. It is really a very human response. When the attraction is there, receipt of information feels more akin to a natural flow than a barrage.

Additionally, attraction operates on a different rhythm than promotion. It feels friendlier, more relaxed. It doesn't come with either the volume or the urgency of promotion. If orchestrated effectively, it can almost feel organic and inevitable.

Elliot Sloane, Senior Managing Director at FTI Consulting, said the U2 Joshua Tree concert in New York City was, to him, a perfect illustration of attraction vs. promotion.

"Bono is a total rock star," said Sloane. "It's funny how that whole vibe he gives off, that glow he radiates that is so irresistible, reminds me of T. Boone Pickens." (*T. Boone Pickens is a well known financier and architect of an energy plan for America, Chairman and Chief Executive Officer of BP Capital.*)

"I worked for Boone for years while at my previous firm. We managed all the earned media for his Pickens Plan. Our goal was to communicate the benefits of getting the US off foreign oil and onto alternative resources – wind, solar, natural gas. I got to know Boone very well during this assignment. He's an incredible guy. Smart. Very very smart. Charismatic. Tireless. A real leader. From humble roots. Boone is the kind of guy who commands the spotlight. Who generates heat by just standing there. Like Bono. Anyway, as his PR guy, I used to marvel at how much the mainstream press – I mean the largest and most complex and hardest to work with press – all wanted to talk to him. The sell wasn't in getting the press *interested*. They were always interested. The work was in figuring out how to choreograph, how to strategize, how to emerge with the results we wanted.

"So why am I going on like this? I used to tell people, without ever having met Bono or without ever even having seen him in concert, that working for Boone was like working for Bono. A pure rock star. A guy who turned heads standing still. A guy who truly operated by the principle that keeps getting beaten into my head – attraction rather than promotion. Working for Boone was like working for Bono. Last night, watching Bono perform, there was the difference between attraction and promotion in action. There was Bono, in his black outfit, his tinted glasses, standing all alone on an extended stage, his band members a few hundred feet behind him...standing all alone, holding his mic, not just standing in his rock star pose, but being a rock star...with his own manner of humility and intellect, attracting his audience, not promoting to it. The emotional buy-in when there's this kind of attraction is incredible. Not surprising, but incredible."

Promotion or being promoted to is far less likely to give you this feeling.

Focusing on creating an attraction among stakeholders to your message, your actions and your initiatives, now that's a different level of effort. And excitement. And satisfaction.

As Mary Lynn Carver, Chief Communications Officer and Global Vice President of General Mills, said to me, "Anyone can have a megaphone." Getting heard and having that message resonate is something else altogether.

GENTLE COLLISIONS: ONE WAY TO CREATE ATTRACTION

I first heard this phrase working with a guy called Michael Markowitz, former Chief Brand Officer at Panera Bread.

He approached our agency for help in finding meaningful intersections for his brand at key moments in its customers' everyday lives when they'd find the brand messages most attractive. He called this a "gentle collision".

Quantitative data he conducted revealed that his customers didn't want to feel 'marketed' to. Reading between the lines, what his customers were saying is that they didn't want his brand, or any other, to be only in their faces. If a brand wanted their trust, their loyalty, and ultimately their dollar, it needed to also get into their lives.

Gentle collisions do just that. They extend a brand's reach through personal and authentic intersections in the everyday lives of the target audience. These naturally strike an emotional chord, meet an everyday need, or deliver something useful in a way that connects in a deeply personal way. Gentle collisions are one way to keep it real.

This strategy complements advertising and other marketing tactics and contributes to brand sales without leaving the customer feeling like they've just been sold. Authentic gentle collisions bring a brand and its creative platform to life in a way that goes well beyond awareness. They create a connection that touches stakeholders in a way that eclipses how they feel about your company, your industry, the price of the products – the kinds of feelings that can sometimes be turn-offs.

Consumers and patients need some semblance of a feeling that a company or a brand knows them and cares about them and their needs, challenges, and aspirations, and is delivering exclusively for them. This approach creates attraction because it requires stakeholders to allow your message, brand or company into their life versus promotion, which pushes itself in their faces.

THE ROADMAP TO GENTLE COLLISIONS THAT CREATE ATTRACTION

Conduct the necessary research. It will provide answers to the questions listed below and show you where to find the gentle collisions in the lives of your stakeholders.

» *Where does your target audience spend time?* The goal of a gentle collision is to provide something that adds value or somehow enhances an experience. We once held a heart-healthy screening in a place called the "World's Largest Laundromat" in Chicago – a non-traditional venue to say the least – but the hub of the local community, which was the target audience.

» *Does your audience need something that takes their mind off an issue or situation that concerns them?* In that case, perhaps your role in the relationship is to be the source of a welcome distraction.

» *Do your audience's concerns need amplification?* What about offering a voice for stakeholders who have a hard time getting heard?

The aim of PR messaging and engagement based on attraction is to convert passive stakeholders into active ones who want to listen to you and want to participate.

CHAPTER 4

CREATIVITY

*"Logic will get you from A to B.
Imagination will take you everywhere."*

Albert Einstein[16]

We received an assignment from a multinational company, a client I'd had for more than 15 years, to design a dashboard for the company's internal PR department. Included were metrics that executives could use to judge brand communications campaigns. These encompassed overall impressions, reach with priority audiences, message penetration, creativity of the approach or communications solution, alignment with other elements in the marketing mix, and line-of-sight to brand goals. The dashboard came back with one change: delete creativity. The reason? Creativity is not a 'must have' for an effective campaign that meets business objectives.

I remember being struck by that. Is creativity now just a 'nice to have?' Is that how little it is valued? Curiosity drove me to do some digging. In very little time, I found an article by influential columnist David Brooks published in the *New York Times* that said creativity had been trumped by the desire to edge out the competition. Competitive "myopia" had taken over, he lamented, undermining innovation.[17]

Jon Iwata, formerly of IBM, appreciates creativity as much as the next executive, but doesn't like to get hung up on how it is defined. "We know the art of human engagement requires thoughtfulness and innovation and, yes, I'd say creativity too."

So why then would my client think creativity is optional? According to a survey of agency and client executives conducted for OMD by *AdAge* and Erdos & Morgan, creativity tops the list of qualities that clients look for in media agencies, closely followed by data and analytics and efficient business processes.[18] While creativity is at the top, these numbers reveal the tightrope that marketers are walking between a desire for innovation and the determination to win. A well and carefully considered creative idea should be able to achieve both.

PR has a rich heritage of clever and effective campaigns that result in better, stronger connections to a company or brand's stakeholders. Sometimes the core of the idea is an unexpected exploitation of a competitor's weakness or an insight that has been hidden in plain sight.

Creativity – especially in service of a reputation build – takes work. You can find a truly original idea if you're honest and unfiltered. As a reality check, though, I also keep in mind what standup comedian Bo Burnham says: "Original doesn't mean good." For me meaning that the bar needs to be higher.

A creative idea also needs to be evidence-based and offer a clear line of sight to business objectives. At Merck, says Michael Blash, Global Head of Internal Communications, you can't just come in with an idea that is only considered 'creative' for the sake of being creative.

Instead he explains, "A truly creative idea needs to be grounded in a business objective along with performance metrics. The creativity needs to move the brand, move the company in some way, and get us closer to meeting our goals."

PR campaigns that generate buzz, change behaviour or become models in the industry typically centre on a creative idea or a creative execution of a brand insight. Creative success breaks the mould, takes us to places we didn't think possible.

It is exciting and requires the discipline to think through a new idea all the way from insight to strategy and then execution. You need to anticipate as many questions and challenges as you can. For example, will your internal and external audiences understand the message? Will it convince customers to choose this brand? Or, in the case of a pharmaceutical brand, will they ask their doctor about it?

Sometimes you have to be ruthless. You need to be willing to scrap an idea that is just plain better on paper than in reality. This happens all the time and I don't find it gets any easier with repetition. It may be comforting to remember that coming up with a creative PR idea requires far more human resources than buying more advertising in a different medium, developing coupons or offering free trials.

Market research, analytics and a tight strategy all have their places as 'must haves' – alongside creativity.

Mark Zuckerberg, founder and Chief Executive Officer of Facebook

"Ideas never come out fully formed. They become so over time, as you work on them."[19]

There are myriad ways to spark creativity. Here are some suggestions:

- Do something creative for two minutes the moment you wake up in the morning. This could be some kind of output which engages free thinking and connections, including writing something, composing a melody, outlining an idea for a lyric, singing an original song in the shower. Elliot Sloane composes a one-minute musical meditation every day. "My morning musical meditation allows me to slow down and get my fingers to unlock the free association that is necessary for problem solving. Some chief executive officers kayak or rock climb to get to the same place. Maybe there's a happiness and satisfaction element that impacts the work."

- Schedule a few minutes some time each day to write. Carl Richards, author of *Want to be Creative on Purpose?*

Schedule it, says this is the exact opposite of waiting for inspiration to strike.[20]

- Find inspirations. They're all around you if you're open to spotting them and then allowing them in.

- Do things out of your comfort zone.

- Read science fiction, watch sci-fi movies. I have a very successful PR friend who swears her best ideas were sparked by these futuristic stories.

- Find quiet time. The inventor Nikola Tesla believed that being alone was the secret of invention. "That is when ideas are born."[21]

- Do nothing. The psychologist Amos Tversky had his own version of this point. "The secret to doing good research is always to be a little underemployed." Another supporter of this method is George Shultz. As reported in a *New York Times* article, when Schultz was secretary of state in the 1980s, he liked to carve out one hour each week for quiet reflection. He sat down in his office with a pad of paper and pen, closed the door and told his secretary to interrupt him only if one of two people called: "My wife or the President." His hour of solitude was the only way he could find time to think about the strategic aspects of his job. Otherwise, he would be constantly pulled into moment-to-moment tactical issues, never able to focus on larger questions of the national interest. And the only way to do great work, in any field, is to find time to consider the larger questions.[22]

Here are a few additional suggestions for leading or participating in a group discussion with the aim of identifying a creative PR solution:

- How to begin? The mantra of every brainstorming session I've sat in over the years is, "There are no bad ideas. Everything is fair game." If you like this, it is a tried and true place to start.

- Ask the question that will dictate how you spend your time for the next hour: Would the challenge you're working on benefit most from a creative idea or solution? If yes, you all stay in the room and do the work of creativity. If not, meeting over.

- Consider an ice-breaker type game to loosen people up so they can get into their 'creative zones', whatever that may look like for them. Typical ice-breakers include 'desert island' (participants write down what music, book and luxury item they would take if stranded on a desert island) or 'two truths and a lie' (each person writes down two truths and a lie about themselves and the group needs to identify the lie).

- Respect but do not be restricted by market research, keeping in mind what Henry Ford said: "If I asked my customers what they wanted, they'd have said a faster horse."

- Consider focusing your creativity on solving an issue of discontent – or as Jerry Seinfeld says, "What am I really sick of?" This is a good starting point for innovative thinking.

- Find a balance of creativity and business objectives within your overall brand strategies.

- Lastly, have plenty of toys on the table that people can play with while they think. Pipe cleaners are popular as are stress balls.

CHAPTER 5

DON'T JUST LISTEN; REALLY HEAR AND INCLUDE

*"Most people do not listen with
the intent to understand;
they listen with the intent to reply."*

Steven R. Covey[23]

For four years, I was the Vice President of Marketing Communications and PR for a start-up medical diagnostics company. Every month, the management team would meet for a 9am-5pm state-of-the-business session. Inevitably, by 10:30am, 12 noon tops, the meeting would become a free-for-all. It was difficult to finish a sentence let alone a presentation without someone interrupting to agree, disagree, build on the thought or bring up a point that was related but on a different track. We all kind of got used to this and just went with the flow. Obviously, this was the culture of this particular company. But, when a new COO joined – he was Canadian and had just completed a stint at a multi-national diagnostics giant – he was appalled at the raucousness of this discussion style and said so. He quickly banned interrupting and, while it lasted, the meeting discussions became not only more pleasant, but a more productive use of time for the entire team.

Listening, really *listening,* and actually hearing each other shouldn't be so difficult, but it is and takes work. Listening requires taking a pause and a step back before responding. This enables the listener to understand why stakeholders feel and act the way they do.

In his book *On Becoming a Person*, psychologist Carl Rogers wrote, "Real communication occurs when we listen with understanding – to see the idea and attitude from the other person's point of view, to sense how it feels to them, to achieve their frame of reference in regard to the thing they are talking about."[24]

The first step is to try to listen more than you talk. This sage advice has been around for thousands of years. Indeed, Zeno of Citium, a Hellenistic thinker from 336-265 BCE, was known to have said, "We have two ears and one mouth, so we should listen more than we say."[25]

As if it were that simple. But it is more worthwhile to attempt to engage with this advice than to ignore it. The benefits of effective listening can be surprising.

LISTENING FOR COLLABORATION AND INNOVATION

Henry Elkus, Chief Executive Officer of Helena – a non-profit organization that convenes world leaders to discuss and implement solutions to global issues – creates the kind of environment in which feedback is solicited and heard from everyone in his company. As a result of this openness, one of Helena's interns dramatically helped improve the direction his organization would take.

"The intern saved me and the rest of our team the wasted time and energy we might have spent continuing down a suboptimal path," Elkus said.[26]

"To solve real-world problems, you need real-world dialogue. That's what PR does best."

Mike Fernandez, Chief Executive Officer, Burson-Marsteller

LISTENING TO YOUR STAKEHOLDERS

Internal PR departments at companies, often along with their agencies, are expected to be the eyes and ears of their organisations. Our backgrounds and training often establish us as the most qualified to serve in this role and advise company leadership accordingly. This skill set is needed on an ongoing basis, but never more than when internal or external stakeholders do not agree with the company's message or a particular action. Listening is the first step in understanding the motivation behind their point of view. The second is to let the insights gleaned help chart the communications course.

"Too often, management come to see opponents, competitors and critics as the enemy, and then spend a lot of time worrying about what they're saying or doing," explains Paul Holmes, Chair of The Holmes Group. "If they're listening properly, PR professionals can see the situation from the point of view of the stakeholder, approach the criticism with empathy and then work out the best path forward."

Listening allows companies to find common ground with critics. It's often more possible than not to devise a PR strategy that shines a spotlight on those areas of agreement while, on a parallel track, the company works to address areas of disconnect or discontent.

LISTENING, IN ALL ITS FORMS

There are many ways to listen during live interactions, whether in person, on the phone or through videochats. Live interactions allow 'listening' with multiple senses for a complete picture that includes the words being used, the tone of voice, body language, interaction with others involved in the exchange, and overall countenance and presentation of the players. I'm reminded here of a court stenographer I once hired to attend a symposium we organized for a client, to deliver a detailed transcript of the presentations. To my surprise, she was completely hard of hearing! She did her job, and an excellent one at that, by lip-reading and through her observations derived from her heightened alternate senses.

Technology also provides us with a variety of tools and services to help us capture listening information more efficiently. Social listening has given us listening scale as well as depth. Data sets that capture digital trends are of the utmost importance to the future of PR, according to a report conducted by the Association of National

Advertisers (ANA) and the USC Center for Public Relations at the Annenberg School for Communication and Journalism.[27]

RESILIENT LISTENING

Listening means inviting people to speak and then actually *hearing* and taking in a variety of points of view which reflect different experiences, contributing factors, and perspectives. This is hard and is getting harder as people become more segmented and everyday issues become more polarized. Now multiply by at least ten the difficulty and effort it takes to respectfully take in different view points on a highly charged, deeply contentious topic and you've arrived at 'resilient listening'.

According to Encounter, a non-partisan educational organization cultivating informed and constructive dialogue about the Israeli-Palestinian conflict, resilient listening allows a person and/or a community to live with tension, to hold multiple perspectives at the same time, and to continue to be open to learning and development, rather than guarding against new ideas and shutting down. Their theory is that only when we can learn from those with whom we disagree can we be more effective and solution-oriented advocates and change-agents.[28]

One may think PR for managing issues in the business world would be far less fraught than the Israeli-Palestinian conflict, and that evaluation is probably right. However, Encounter's philosophy is a useful model when collecting the information and then devising a strategy for companies or organizations that need to forge relationships with critics, or those who do not share their point of view. Resilient listening can create an environment in which conflicting perspectives can be shared, so that a foundation for moving forward can be honestly considered.

The perils of not listening and of not hearing other viewpoints are obvious. Experiments at the University of Michigan revealed that, when challenged with a difficult problem, groups composed of highly adept members performed *worse* than groups whose members had varying levels of skill and knowledge. The reason for this, seemingly, is directly linked to a lack of diverse thinking. Group members who think alike or who are trained in similar disciplines with parallel knowledge bases run the risk of becoming insular. Instead of exploring alternatives, they allow a confirmation bias to take over and tend to reinforce each other's predispositions.

INCLUSION

> "I don't think we're
> really listening
> unless we're willing
> to be changed by
> the other person."
>
> Alan Alda[29]

Stepping back, it is disheartening to see that we live in a deeply divided society today. Tolerance and a willingness to learn appear to be increasingly scarce, not to mention our growing reluctance to embrace the diversity of each other's experiences and opinions.

"Companies lose employees when they don't feel heard, when they don't feel they have a valuable voice in the work environment. It's not enough to invite them in and ask them what they think. They need to feel that their opinions and points of view matter," maintains Helen Shelton, Senior Partner at Finn Partners.

It is not possible to overstate the benefits of listening for inclusion. Mike Fernandez, Chief Executive Officer at

Burson-Marsteller, told me a story about his experience during his six-year tenure leading global corporate affairs at Cargill, the world's largest privately held company and one of the world's leading producers and marketers of food, agricultural, financial and industrial products and services. He was responsible for communications, brand and marketing services, government relations, and corporate social responsibility.

"In the late 1990s, there was an overwhelming desire *not* to have GMOs in Europe, despite the benefits. Oddly enough, environmental groups got behind that. This forced soy farmers in Italy and France out of business and then European manufacturers of certain food and personal care products dependent on soy needed to find other sources.

"The number one producer of soy in the world is the United States but virtually all of its soy is generated from genetically modified seeds.

"The world's second largest producer of soy is Brazil. Non-GMO soy was growing west of Sao Paulo. Unfortunately, there was GMO soy growing nearby too. Fearing that seeds and products would be co-mingled, manufacturers looked North to Mato Grosso and the Amazon biome. The non-GMO soy became a big market and farmers and ranchers were very eager to plant more acreage, which led to many clearing forests they should not have. This led many of the very same environmental groups, such as Greenpeace, to complain about the Non-GMO farms in Brazil, and they worked with the government to shut down processors including Cargill.

"The team at Cargill was asked to deliver a response and a plan. We said to ourselves and our Cargill management that, before we advanced our own agenda, we first needed to have a conversation with various environmental groups including Greenpeace and others who were critical. Those dialogues were very fruitful, left all parties feeling heard, and led to what is called the Soy Moratorium. As a result of this, Cargill agreed it would not buy soy from farmers that cleared a major amount of land before an agreed date and also agreed to work with farmers to mitigate labour issues. The Soy Moratorium was so successful it became the model.

"Cargill also worked with its competitors and a Brazilian trade group called ABIOVE. Cargill had a separate conversation with environmental groups and agreed they would send satellite imagery of the farms they were doing business with to ensure they weren't monkeying with the agreement. Fast forward several years, the national Brazilian government decided to update its Forest Code and, as part of it, they accepted the principles of the Soy Moratorium. Many people in the industry said this was great at first blush, though thought it would be administered by the government. Environmental groups and larger customers like McDonalds became concerned about whether the Brazilian government would enforce the laws. So, Cargill created a Learning Journey. We called all the various parties, documented their concerns and then took representatives from the various groups – farmers, customers, government officials, and competitors – and went to each of the sites, shared the data and had a conversation to agree that we would continue with the Soy Moratorium.

"This approach did not push an agenda or engage in a one-way promotion of a single message, or single point of view, albeit a powerful one. Instead, by actively seeking and then including other voices and considering many, sometimes opposing, points of view, it was possible to identify areas of mutual agreement for an enduring model."

This is just one example of many. The point is that listening allows for true inclusion. Listening and really hearing lets in all points of view and helps ensure they land on a receptive audience, are considered and truly contribute to the communications solution, such as the company culture, if internally-focused listening, or to messaging if external. This process should not feel like a struggle. This should be natural and organic and moving forward; based on my experience with Millennials, I am confident it will be.

Want to improve your listening? Emma Seppala Ph.D. (Science Director of Stanford University's Center for Compassion and Altruism Research and Education and author of *The Happiness Track*) and Jennifer Stevenson (Vice President of Client Services at TLEX, Transformational Leadership for Excellence) have these suggestions for active listening:

- Be genuinely curious and interested in what is being said, even if initially you're not convinced by the idea being offered.

- Pay attention to cues: does the person spend a lot of time on a particular point?

- Ask yourself, do they get more animated at specific junctures and less so at others?

Listening more and with true curiosity not only helps you to better connect and understand what is being said, but also provides valuable input on how you may frame your response and navigate the conversation. It can help you tune into the topics your colleague is passionate about. Getting to know them will help you understand their perspective and come to an agreement that meets everyone's needs.

CHAPTER 6

WORDS
ARE OUR
CURRENCY

"Words are loaded pistols."

Jean-Paul Sartre[30]

That old adage about a picture being worth a thousand words is often true. An expression on someone's face may reveal a sudden truth. A well-known politician caught on camera in a compromising position can forever change his or her reputation. There are many situations in which seeing is believing. This idea reminds me of the expression, 'the best PR involves being caught (literally, visually) in the act of doing something good.'

That said, words remain incredibly powerful, whether spoken or written. They make strong and lasting impressions on the listener or the reader in everyday life and professionally.

Consider this situation. A PR friend recently recounted an anecdote about when she worked with a physician spokesperson on a media tour to share data about a new cancer medication. After a great deal of planning, pitching and reference-providing, she finally scored a slot for the doctor on a much-coveted, national news show. To prepare for the interview, the PR team took the physician through extensive training, anticipating as many questions as possible, and removing all the "umms" and unnecessary gesticulations from the doctor's presentation style. During the interview, which was live, the doctor was asked a question about whether the medication extended a patient's life – a question covered in the training – yet on live TV, when it was heard by millions, the doctor said, "I can't speak to that, but I suppose everybody needs to die someday."

Mic drop.

This was decidedly *not* the answer the doctor had prepared and practiced, and not something anybody expected to fly from her lips. And those last five words – which probably took up four seconds in an otherwise very articulate, professionally delivered, highly valuable interview – were all anybody remembered. And not for a good reason.

Words matter. They always have. And they always will.

AVOID JARGON

Every industry has a set of vocabulary, or jargon, associated with it. Typically, people outside that particular space have no idea what the jargon means and this can result in recipient frustration which may lead to tuning out, or immediately hitting the 'delete' button. Here is a good example of jargon at its worst, recently posted by an executive on LinkedIn:

"I received an email from a company that plans pay-for-play conferences and they want access to our clients as an audience (and the associated revenue) for their events. I usually just delete such messages, but for some reason I replied to this one. My reply read: *'Can you tell me who you are and what you do?'*

"The respondent answered: *"We provide a platform for market-moving dialogue by connecting decision makers through actionable exchange, revolutionizing the way 21st century companies create value. When can we talk?"'*

Any idea what the offer was? I don't either.

While there are always 'it' words that seem to catch on and find resonance, and it absolutely make sense to note these, we should use them sparingly. It is inevitable that they will get overused and eventually become hackneyed phrases, to the point that their meaning is anyone's guess.

It is fine to invent a new word or turn of phrase you can associate with a brand or company (more on this below), but, otherwise, I advise the use of clean language, well-chosen words, and simple, well articulated messaging.

Interestingly, Webster is adding new words at a rapid pace because of social media. Now, more than ever, brand new expressions and words are infiltrating the vernacular.

DEVELOP A LEXICON WHEN YOU HAVE THE OPPORTUNITY

Advertising is often credited with creating new vocabulary about a particular brand or topic. Snappy copy, memorable taglines, and lots of repetition contribute to this success. How often have you used the phrase "Just do it" for virtually any effort where a little extra motivation is needed? We all have our favourites. But PR can also play a critical role in establishing a new lexicon through well-placed and effectively timed media coverage, everyday engagement, and efficient campaigns.

This is particularly evident in healthcare communications. For example, for a medication that works via a novel mechanism of action, it is essential to offer language patients can relate to and genuinely understand. Successful use of such language can carve out a distinctive position. New language, perhaps first revealed in advertising, also needs to be presented by, and accessible through, trusted sources. The lexicon gets a different treatment in PR vehicles. It becomes less commercial and more credible, permitting patients and consumers to feel comfortable using it themselves among friends and family, or in conversations with physicians. PR, working independently – or better still, as part of a well-integrated team of agencies from other disciplines – brings the vocabulary to life through the myriad outlets we use so effectively.

Consider a disease state that many feel is too 'private' to talk about, such as vaginal atrophy or erectile dysfunction. Or take the instance of a condition that can be misunderstood (very high triglycerides) because it is overshadowed by a more established condition (high cholesterol). What about illnesses that may have a stigma attached to them (depression)? Some highly treatable health problems go untreated because patients and their families or caregivers don't have effective or non-threatening or 'inoffensive' words to describe the symptoms. Developing vocabulary people can use and then gently but effectively easing it into everyday vernacular and circumstances can make the difference between silent suffering and productive action.

Well-conceived and effectively executed PR has contributed to the successful introduction and use of socially acceptable language for a variety of situations. Considering the growing importance of stakeholder segmentation, it may be even more likely that no one vocabulary fits all.

Geographic, socio-economic, cultural, and demographic differences will dictate the words to use that will best communicate information about an issue or brand to particular stakeholders. PR has the flexibility and the tactical arsenal to make a new lexicon about a difficult subject relatable, no matter where the target audience is ideologically positioned. But this can only be the case if we have the words.

WORDS THAT RESONATE WITH STAKEHOLDERS

Words and phrases can trigger emotions. Different meanings and feelings can be attributed to words, depending on a variety of factors such as geography, age, culture – pop or past – or can be defined according to a specific point of reference. When building relationships with stakeholders, you need to be aware of these factors to determine the words that will land best for that particular group or purpose.

In the classes I teach as part of the Brand and Integrated Communications graduate program at City College in New York, I play all kinds of word games. One favourite exercise in learning how to communicate clearly and with empathy is when I partner students and ask them to tell each other a brief anecdote from their lives (the story must be true) that is particularly meaningful to them for one reason or another. Then, each student has to retell the other's story to the entire class in a way that places the speaker in their partner's shoes and conveys the appropriate emotion. This forces students to take themselves out of the equation and avoid filtering someone else's story through their own experience and vocabulary. Instead it requires them to listen carefully for the words and the emotions being conveyed and then channel that experience.

GOOD WORDS ARE EVERYWHERE

Words are all around us. You find them online, in social media, on billboards, in your emails, and in books – new and old.

Reading is an excellent way to learn new words and turns of phrase. I will never forget a '60 Minutes' interview I saw with the rapper Eminem, in which he told interviewer Anderson Cooper that he regularly reads the dictionary to find ways to rhyme. He writes down words he learns and thinks of this as "stacking ammo". Maybe he was thinking of the Sartre quote I used to open this chapter when he made that statement? Anyway, my favourite part of this interview was when he said it "pissed him off" that people think you can't find a rhyme for the word orange. And then he proceeded to give examples.[31] The point he was making is that words are there for the taking. When you need them, they can be found and learned and, most importantly, used to your benefit, to forward your cause and strengthen your point.

Clips of this interview are available on YouTube. Well worth watching, if only to learn what rhymes with orange!

Try reading the dictionary like Eminem. It has always been a fantastic and super-accessible resource. I confess that I do not read the dictionary, but I pull a new word from dictionary.com every day and see if I can use it in a sentence I either say or write.

If, unlike Eminem, reading the dictionary does not appeal to you, then find another way to engage with new words and language. Simply get into the habit of writing down words that catch your attention. The 'Notes' tool of most smartphones or a similar app is a handy place to archive these. When you encounter a new word, look it up. Try it out on your own – in speaking, in writing. Note the way you feel when you use it. Observe how it lands on your audience. If it feels good to you personally and strikes a positive note, use it again.

Listen carefully to the way people you admire speak. Capture those words and phrases you like, that you remember well. After a couple of weeks at her first internship at a PR agency, one of my students said she loved the way her boss spoke, even though she wasn't familiar with some of the words used. I encouraged her to record the words and phrases on her smartphone as soon as she heard them and then look them up later. Once she got in the habit of doing this, her comprehension improved, as did her own vocabulary. As an additional benefit, she had even more admiration for her boss than she'd had before! I first got into the habit of writing down words and expressions I heard as an account executive at Ruder Finn. David Finn, the Chief Executive Officer at the time and long considered a pioneer in PR, used some particularly rich and colourful phrases and words, several of which I still use today (and I always credit him when I do so).

Make an effort to grow your vocabulary. This is a daily practice, a little like yoga, which stretches your brain and allows more flexibility with language. I promise, this sort of engagement with words never gets old; quite the opposite: it will keep your ideas and mind fresh.

Reading is my favourite way to build vocabulary that improves writing and the ability to articulate ideas. Here are a few additional suggestions that are reliable and fun:

Scrabble®[32]: Have a dictionary or your phone with the dictionary app close by.

Hangman: This has always been my go-to travelling game, used when my children were young and fidgety, especially on stalled New York City subways. We still play.

Bananagrams®[33]: A great game that is easy to transport and it comes in a yellow banana-shaped bag.

Divide Quotes: I learned this game from my friend Monica one Thanksgiving. Since then, I've introduced it to students in my classes. It's a great way to introduce interesting turns of phrase. For this game, I research famous quotations and then divide each into two separate parts that I write on individual slips of paper. I fold up each slip and put them all in a cup and shake them up. Then each person selects a slip. The first person announces their phrase and it is up to the holders of the remaining slips to figure out if the phrase they have completes the one announced. Proceed around the room until all the quotations are complete.

Six word stories: I ask students to tell a complete happy (or a sad) story in six words. We also often play this game with five words. This teaches word choice and brevity.

Word of the Day by Merriam Webster: One of the many virtually effortless ways to learn a new word is to have one literally delivered to your smartphone everyday. Go immediately to Merriam Webster's Word of the Day. You can learn more here: https://www.merriam-webster.com/word-of-the-day. The *New York Times* offers a new word that has been used recently in published articles plus a quiz to test understanding. Here is a link: https://www.nytimes.com/column/learning-word-of-the-day.

CHAPTER 7

INSPIRE
TO CHANGE
BEHAVIOR

"I've learned that people will forget what you said, people will forget what you did, but people will never forget how you made them feel."

Maya Angelou[34]

I tend to actually make good on my New Year's Resolutions in May and early June. This is, in large part, because the internet and my social feeds become filled with YouTube videos of speeches from university commencements. The inspiration I feel from these can turn even my months-old lofty aspirations into action.

Among the many powerful speeches, some really stand out. One is the 2014 "Make your bed" address delivered at the University of Texas at Austin by Admiral William H. McRaven,[35] that has since been turned into a best-selling book by the same name.[36] And I can tell you that since hearing this former Navy Seal's speech, I have made my bed every day at home, on vacation and even in hotel rooms. Admiral McRaven's message is that it is possible to change the world by committing to do the small things – even seemingly inconsequential tasks – like making your bed every day, with a real commitment, real discipline.

Steve Jobs' speech at Stanford University in 2005 also remains with me as an inspirational message of hope, self-knowledge and perseverence.[37] Mark Zuckerberg spoke at Harvard in 2017 and, while he started off a bit slowly, in my opinion, he finished strongly and memorably on the issue of social change and how every individual can contribute.[38]

And then there are the thoughts Bill Gates posted to graduates in 2017. In his message, he recommends a book by Steven Pinker called, *The Better Angels of Our Nature*[39] and concludes with the power of belief in what's possible.

"Pinker makes a persuasive argument that the world is getting better, that we are living in the most peaceful time in human history. This can be a hard case to make, especially now. When you tell people the world is improving, they often look at you like you're either naive or crazy. But it's true. And once you understand it, you start to see the world differently. If you think things are getting better, then you want to know what's working so you can accelerate the progress and spread it to more people and places. It doesn't mean you ignore the serious problems we face. It just means you believe they can be solved, and you're moved to act on that belief."[40]

That last sentence is everything. If it is possible to encourage people to believe something can be solved, then they are moved to take action. Giving people a reason to believe a problem – their problem – can be solved inspires action. Simply put, what Pinker and Gates are suggesting is that *hope* is what drives action.

PR is often enlisted to help change behaviour or create a 'call to action'. The action could be anything from seeking information, visiting a website, downloading a coupon, participating in a contest, 'liking' a social post, sharing a video, talking to a professional – such as a doctor in the case of healthcare PR programmes – beginning a new dialogue or changing the dialogue, following a healthier lifestyle, buying a product, or considering a different point of view. All these actions, and many others besides, are actions that can precipitate real change.

There has been a great deal written about the value and success of motivation for changing behaviour. Susan Fowler, professor at the University of San Diego and best-selling author, wrote a book called *Why Motivating People Doesn't Work and What Does: The New Science of Leading, Energizing and Engaging*. She believes there are many reasons motivation doesn't work. One is that motivation is an "inside out phenomenon", making enforced change from the outside almost impossible, if the internal motivation is missing. Another reason it is so challenging is because people are "already motivated. They just may not be motivated the way you want them to be motivated".[41]

'Motivation' has become kind of a throwaway word to me. Many PR briefs, especially in healthcare (the space I've primarily worked in for over 30 years), ask for a strategy and activations that motivate stakeholders to do something. This could be to make healthier food choices, exercise more, lose weight, assess one's risks for a condition, talk to the doctor about symptoms or a specific treatment or visit a brand website. The problem is that, in my experience, so-called motivation doesn't actually *motivate*. Something else does.

Some suggest that fear and guilt are strong motivators and that these emotions should underpin strategies when motivation is the endgame. For example, by reminding those who need to check on and improve their heart health that they need to do so if they want to be fit (and for 'fit' read: alive) to walk down the aisle at their daughter's wedding or to play with their grandchildren. There's a pretty unsubtle threat of, 'or else' here. Many believe this is effective, and perhaps it is, based on the sheer number of ads I've seen, PR programmes I've observed, and quotes in press releases that follow this approach.

Based on years of observation and data that scare tactics are often ineffective at instigating behavioural change, my preference, and often my recommendation to clients, is to consider an alternative approach. Here is a formula that can be considered for those PR challenges that ask for a call to action or a behaviour change:

Give hope + a practical roadmap for turning hope into a trial process that can be repeated and leads to habit.

If this seems viable to you in relation to the PR challenge you're working on, the following are some steps to consider:

1. When your goal is to create a behaviour or thought change, or a call-to-action, begin your process with a deep understanding of your stakeholders. Do the research so you understand their emotional triggers and day-to-day lives and challenges.

2. Find your own empathy. Remember that you – the real you, not the PR person you project – have something in common with the people you need to communicate with. Bring your humanity to the table.

3. Find the higher truth in your message that makes people *want* to take the action you are asking of them. This is more human, less commercial and certainly less promotional. This higher truth, what we sometimes refer to as the 'higher calling' is at the top of the message pyramid and is what your stakeholders will find most relatable and most attractive.

There is real brain chemistry in the connection between higher purpose and positive behaviour. According to economist and psychologist Paul Zak, "Experiments show that having a sense of higher purpose stimulates oxytocin production, as does trust. Trust and purpose then mutually reinforce each other, providing a mechanism for extended oxytocin release, which produces happiness." If you want to read more about this, take a look at an article from the *Harvard Business Review* called, "The Neuroscience of Trust."[42]

4. Often, successful asks or calls-to-action address a discontent or a frustration that is current and on the minds of your stakeholders. As with all the suggestions in this book, this is an idea, not a rule. Your ask needs to be dictated by your research and the challenge at hand.

5. Whatever the ask is, make it achievable and keep the language you use simple. There shouldn't be any ambiguity. After all, how easy is it to remember to "make your bed" every day?

6. The ask should be positive and make people who take the action feel good about themselves in some way: physically, culturally, spiritually or professionally, as contributors to society or their community.

7. Consider who does the asking. The source of the ask is extremely important. Who is the spokesperson, the source of the voice of your campaign? Is he or she credible and trusted? Most decisions to change behaviour or take an action do not require extensive research. People make decisions such as these based on trust.

8.   Create a sense of community where people can make their action personal and share their experiences. You can aim to spark a movement or crusade.

Ideally, the action will become a habit, which will eventually turn into a value. And then your PR effort will be a success.

"Your beliefs become
your thoughts,
Your thoughts become
your words,
Your words become
your actions,
Your actions become
your habits,
Your habits become
your values,
Your values become
your destiny."

Mahatma Gandhi[43]

CHAPTER 8

WHY NOT?

EMBRACE CHANGE

"Everything comes to him who hustles while he waits."

Thomas Edison[44]

Like any service function or service industry, PR needs to regularly assert itself as a valuable – no, make that an invaluable – resource. It is an ongoing process. As my business partner, Jeremy, relentlessly reminds me, "We're only as good as our next performance." While I'm sure someone else even more famous said that line first, it is a mantra that has propelled us for more than 30 years.

So, in that vein, if one of the following applies to you, I applaud you.

That wildly successful brand launch you engineered last year? Impressive!

Your deft handling last month of critical stakeholders during the manufacturing crisis? Well done!

The top industry PR award you won last night for that public service campaign? Congratulations!

By all means, be proud of yourself and your team. Enjoy these moments. Write up those case studies! Learn from these successes and then write articles for industry publications and give talks to industry peers so you can share these gains in learning. Celebrate with your peers and family.

But, after all that, put them behind you and focus on looking ahead to what's next. What else is needed? What PR challenge haven't you met yet? How else can you contribute your unique and increasingly powerful PR skills to your organization or company or client?

Standing still is not an option. Complacency is your enemy.

This may appear to be a harsh assessment, but it is more positive and far more exciting to view this reality as an opportunity. Or even as a gift. Embracing the chance for change and development will encourage you to push boundaries and scale new heights.

Accepting that you will need to constantly demonstrate and prove the need for (and the value of) our discipline, thereby stretching it as you go, will contribute mightily toward cementing PR's reputation, and also your own.

STRETCH...OR ELSE

Service businesses redefine themselves all the time. PR agencies merge with other PR agencies and agencies with specialties such as public affairs, lobbying firms and speaker trainers. Media agencies buy consultancies. Consider the movements of consultancies Accenture and Deloitte. Accenture, formerly known as Andersen Consulting, "reinvented, rebirthed and repositioned" itself into a powerhouse of business solutions that now includes creative content and campaigns, digital and social marketing and, most recently, advertising. Indeed, consultancies are "rushing to get into the ad business," according to *AdWeek* and are striving to help clients with everything from web design to product development.[45]

This new reality is keeping ad agency leaders awake at night, as they are forced to devise strategies for managing a constant influx of new and formidable competitors.

"The big consultancies are underestimating the value of creativity [and] the agencies are under-exploiting the value of business analytics," said Ivan Pollard, former Senior Vice President of strategic marketing at Coca-Cola North America in an article in *AdAge*. "Someone's going to crack that soon because data plus creativity is the future."[46]

Watching this situation unfold for the ad world, a question I've asked myself is: Could another equation for the future be data plus creativity plus PR? And, if so, will consultancies soon be adding PR to their mix? And, if so, what will happen to PR?

I posed this question to Jon Iwata and he said, "Marketing, human resources and other professions are adopting techniques and methods that resemble what we do in PR. This is understandable, even inevitable, because we're all trying to engage and influence people's perceptions and ultimately their behaviour. But PR stewards the character of the company and uniquely looks across all stakeholders and audiences – all the people who matter to our company. That is a unique and important role, and it should never be confused or blurred with the work of adjacent professions."

Iwata strongly believes it is critical for PR and communications to stay independent and not be absorbed into marketing or other functions. If that were to happen, he feels something very important and very necessary to businesses would be lost. But, even as he states this, he acknowledges that missions change, needs shift, the conversations among stakeholders take different forms and different tones; media and influence gets consumed differently.

This PR space is not 'ours' without an ongoing dynamism, business acumen and real Effort (this is not a typo – Effort, in this context, comes with a capital E).

EMBRACE IT

There are many ways to stay nimble. To keep matters simple, I suggest a question and an answer.

Here is a question to ask yourself on a regular basis: "Why not?" This challenge could mean, why not try something new? Why not do something differently? Why not take on something you haven't done before? Why not look at a situation through a new lens? If you're an agency, why not look at your business with fresh eyes? Why not try to grow a new practice? Why not pivot?

This is not to say that the tried and true processes and methods aren't valuable; that what has been successful before can be successful again; the old adage, 'If it ain't broke, don't fix it' still has a place. What has gone before has tremendous learning value. This point of view will always be a truth, a North Star. But these truths should also be a place to start rather than being treated as the default destination.

The message I want to leave you with here is that getting stuck isn't a viable business or career option. Stretching is good. Embracing the need to stay flexible keeps you on your front foot, and therefore open to progress. Your clients, your business and your work will benefit.

"You see things; and you say 'Why?' But I dream things that never were; and I say 'Why not?'"

George Bernard Shaw[47]

If a problem or question leaves you stuck, then here's the answer: the 'yes' attitude.

A 'yes' mindset is a positive mindset, an open approach. It demonstrates a willingness to listen, consider and include. 'Yes' conveys a sense of teamwork and leadership. 'Yes' means you're eager to learn. A 'yes' suggests you're willing to change your own mind, which is very important when trying to change the minds of others.

'Yes' creates an environment in which creativity and productive discussion – and eventually consensus – can be found.

In short, 'yes' is a foundation upon which to build.

Again, it is absolutely vital to emphasize here that 'yes' is not, under any circumstances, the right answer to everything.

Indeed, there are many circumstances in which 'yes' may be inappropriate, including if you are ever asked to compromise your integrity, or the integrity of the brand, executive or organization, or if you are encouraged to take on an assignment in an impossible time frame, or at an inappropriate budget. Or if you're ever asked to apply your PR skills to a task that requires something else. I want to be clear here: there are many circumstances in PR in which 'yes' is *not* the right answer.

Agility is the new normal – not only for PR, but also for marketing, advertising, consulting, and business as a whole. Our success is no longer based on how clever or effective we've been, but how adept we'll be at what's next, especially given the 24/7 world in which we are operating and the real time of communications. Standing still will lead to stasis; it's only by moving forward and remaining adaptable that we can evolve at the same speed as the world around us.

FIND SOMEONE TO 'BUG YOU'

During my interview for the role of vice president of marketing and communications at the start-up medical diagnostics company, the hard-charging chief executive officer told me he wanted someone with a "fire burning in her belly". Someone, he said, who went to bed every night thinking about how to help the company and leapt up at first light of day with a cracking new idea. I didn't say anything at the time but I distinctly remember thinking that I'd get back to him if I thought of anyone who met that description.

Somehow, I got the job. The secret to landing it and then succeeding at building positive relationships with organizations and key opinion leaders that had never before partnered with the private sector, was listening (and quelling my natural instinct to respond) to what the chief executive officer was asking for in a new member of his executive team. I accepted his challenge, and let it motivate me to new levels.

In my current favourite book, *Misbehaving, The Making of Behavioral Economics*, author and Nobel Prize winner and behavioural economist, Richard Thaler writes about a PhD student, Shlomo Bernartzl, who mastered the fine art of bugging him. Whenever Thaler said he was too busy, or just couldn't think about a new idea or a new project right then, Shlomo would persist. He'd call every couple of months and say, "Are we ready to work now?" As a result of Shlomo's "bugging", as well as a "fountain of interesting ideas", Thaler reports he's written more papers with Shlomo than with anyone else.[48]

Everyone can use this kind of bugging. Find your Shlomo.

CHAPTER 9

NEVER FORGET, IT'S BUSINESS

"It's not personal, Sonny.
It's strictly business."

The Godfather[49]

"It's strictly business." What a line! It's one of the most enduring and oft-quoted statements from Francis Ford-Coppola's iconic movie, *The Godfather*. And while I've never found it to be an absolute in every aspect of above-board business (compared to the Corleone family business which was decidedly more menacing than olive oil), it is a good reminder that the relationships and reputations we are building through effective and often creative communications are in the service of business objectives.

Kelly McGinnis, Senior Vice President and Chief Communications Officer at Levi Strauss & Co. put it this way: "First and foremost, the role of PR here is to help the company accelerate growth – whether that means differentiation of our philosophy, our approach, our brands or protection of our reputation. Stakeholder relationships and influencers, employee alignment – this is all within our PR role."

The growing number of channels available to us, together with the potential of instantaneous sharing, has only increased the alignment of PR and business. A corporate reputation can be negatively impacted, if not significantly damaged, with just one viral video or tweet from an influencer, someone with a significant social media following. The fallout can go straight to the bottom line in a nanosecond. Look no further than the share price plummet of United Airlines, after a passenger was forcefully dragged out of his seat to make room for a commuting crew member. The incident occurred on 9 April, 2017. Two days later, *Forbes* ran a story with the headline, "How United Became the World's Most Hated Airline in One Day."[50] Within a month, a Harris Poll reported that negative perceptions of United Airlines' corporate reputation had increased by 500% and that 42% of U.S. consumers said United had a "bad" or "very bad" reputation.[51] United eventually settled a lawsuit with the passenger for an undisclosed sum, but managing the various repercussions from the backlash took months. A quick Google search yields hundreds of stories about this incident, a good reminder that the internet is forever.

Crisis situations have always demanded considered but timely communications solutions, and PR has been at the centre of these resolutions. The various levels of impact on corporate reputation and the business (e.g. sales, revenue, customer perception) are paramount in these situations.

The same holds true for what might be considered more 'day-to-day' PR for internal and external audiences, as well as creative campaigns, albeit without the tension of a crisis. Even when a company does not appear to be on the verge of catastrophe, reputation is still the key to success and positive communications solutions can help to develop a favourable public perception.

"I don't talk to my staff a lot about our functional capabilities – I talk about our influence on the business."

Kelly McGinnis,
Senior Vice President and Chief
Communications Officer, Levi Strauss & Co.

Mary Lynn Carver, Chief Communications Officer and Global Vice President of General Mills, maintains that, "What has always drawn me to PR is how connected it is to all ends of the business. It's like a giant puzzle – you get to place the different pieces together and are one of the first people to stand back and make the connections. It's a pleasure to be able to see how things fit together." Here, she clearly articulates the crucial role that effective PR plays and the impact that continuous positive involvement can have across all levels and facets of the company.

INTERNAL COMMUNICATIONS

PR teams often work closely with Human Resources departments on internal communications. This transmission of company information between organizational leadership throughout other parts of the organization requires careful planning for an overarching strategy as well as the tactics that bring the strategy to life, including the potential impact of the frequency, content and style of executive team interaction with employees. Letters to employees, emails and speeches from the chief executive officer and others in the C-suite often find their way into the media, whether deliberately or not.

Practitioners of internal PR need to show how their work links back to positive business performance. One way to measure this is to take communications performance metrics and connect them directly to business performance.

"We need to show how communications contribute to the bottom line," says Michael Blash, Global Head of Internal Communications at Merck. "We're held to a similar standard as other channels, such as direct marketing, and therefore need to measure our contributions accordingly."

There are many excellent examples of internal communications that show a clear link to business objectives. Starbucks is often commended for its relationship with employees and the philosophy that governs its messages and tactics. Warby Parker made a big splash with its approach to internal communications and employee practices that had a direct impact on its corporate reputation. Speeches and letters to employees from Satya Nadella, Chief Executive Officer of Microsoft, are well-worth reading. One example that stands out is his email to employees on his first day on the job, which engineers and fosters a positive attitude from the outset.[52]

EXTERNAL COMMUNICATIONS

It is crucial to understand the role of PR in advancing a company's business. PR helps articulate what the company or a brand stands for as well as the benefits to society beyond their own bottom line. This is one important way in which PR differs from marketing.

Dave Samson, General Manager of Public Affairs at Chevron, views what he and his team do for their business in this way: "I have always looked at communications as a business-enabling role, and if it's not just pushing information out, disseminating info or even to drive dialogue – communications should drive action favourable to the companies' interests."

Having expertise in communications strategy and execution – both the art and the craft – as well as business acumen will go a long way. In other words, it's not enough simply to write a decent sentence or 'be creative', to be especially adept at social media or to have 'insights'. I am not disparaging these skills in any way. They are all important and truly valuable skills. My point is simply that the *art* of PR demands that we take a holistic approach to learning about the companies or organizations we're supporting. The rationale for this is simple. To be as effective as possible, PR cannot exist in a 'bubble' or be 'parachuted in' on an ad-hoc basis, simply for a launch or a crisis. In any case, the holistic approach I'm suggesting should be a natural product of the field in which we work.

"To solve real-world problems, you need to engage in real-world dialogue. That's what PR does best."

Mike Fernandez,
Chief Executive Officer,
Burson-Marstellar

Here are some suggestions for maintaining a direct line of sight to business objectives when developing PR strategies:

1. **Understand the overall space in which your company or organization is operating.** This includes understanding the issues and challenges, critics and supporters. Also know your competitors and any other organizations or companies that overlap with yours, or are directly engaging with your stakeholders.

2. **Learn about your company, your products and/or offerings, even if you're not specifically working on any assignments for them individually.** This includes knowing the communities impacted by your

company or products and the views and feelings of employees across the company, as well as investor and governance needs and requirements.

3. **Understand what other people 'at the table' in your company do and their specific challenges and objectives.** Knowing the perspectives of decision makers helps you understand the positioning of the PR role within the overall mix. It also helps guide you on how best to situate and frame your recommendations. Finally, this awareness will enable you to help your peers and colleagues articulate the communications messages that you develop.

4. **Build relationships with your peers and colleagues in other areas of the company.** This will give you a broad perspective. PR is always stronger if you're able to execute communications skills and influence across the business as a whole. This approach to relationships also ensures a steady flow of the kind of information that will help you choose the most appropriate channels and will offer valuable insights into what type of communication activity is needed at various points (for example, when Corporate Social Responsibility activities are necessary).

5. **Have a line of sight to business objectives to help focus creativity and channel selection.** My point here is to encourage PR practitioners not to fall in love with a creative idea simply because it is 'creative' or uses an interesting and exciting channel. Do not imagine a concept will be more valuable or influential

just because it uses the latest engagement channels and technologies, such as virtual reality. Novelty is not necessarily a measure of value or effectiveness. It is important to ensure that the creativity or use of the new tool is not simply a gimmick, but is functioning as part of a larger business objective.

6. **Keep learning.** Many companies and agencies offer training and classes, either on-site or at local universities or organizations. If yours does not, then seek out ways to learn on your own. Sometimes companies or organizations will either contribute a portion of the cost of a class, or find other ways to support the professional development of their workers. There is always value to taking courses that will enhance PR and communication skills, such as writing and public speaking. The same is true of courses that teach about specific tactics, channels or tools such as influencer strategies. But why not also expose yourself to other types of information such as business strategy, business management, behavioural psychology, philosophy and understanding the role of shareholders and the investment community?

This holistic approach ensures that your PR strategies are nuanced and encompass the complexities and needs of the organization.

CHAPTER 10

PERFECTION
IS OVERRATED

"Don't let the perfect be the enemy of the good."

Voltaire[53]

In an interview with the *Harvard Business Review*, the actor Alan Alda was asked about his reputation as a perfectionist. He replied, "I don't think I'm a perfectionist. My early training as an improviser got me used to the idea of uncertainty and the value of the imperfect. Everything is a stepping stone to something else, whether it's perfect or lousy. I'm always looking to get better. It will never be perfect."[54]

Everyone who has ever worked in PR – perhaps every human being who has ever worked with other human beings – has a war story about an event or a situation or a meeting that was memorably imperfect. The result may still have been successful, or successful enough, but that one element kept it from being *perfect*.

Here's one of mine:

I had an annual assignment with a longstanding pharmaceutical company client. My group was responsible for creating the theme and building the educational programme for a three-day off-site symposium with executives from the managed care industry and the company's own extended team. This symposium was an effective and much anticipated programme for relationship-building and creating an environment of learning for both the company sponsor and its stakeholders. My group needed to conduct extensive research to identify the hot topics on the minds of our target audience and then recruit four or five speakers who could address the variety of issues involved.

One speaker we targeted was very in-demand that year. He was a consultant at a top firm, had just been published in an influential journal, was extremely knowledgeable on the most burning issue facing our audience and was generally very well regarded. After a persuasive pitch and some luck, he agreed to be our keynote speaker.

Upon meeting the consultant at the symposium check-in while attendees were arriving, he was everything I'd hoped: bright, articulate, enthusiastic about his role and chatty with clients and symposium participants. My agency colleagues and I were quietly exchanging congratulatory high-fives.

Then, that evening, at the social event before the meeting was to start the next day, we noticed our guy drinking more than seemed appropriate. It was only a matter of time before he got sloppy and then before we knew it, he was relieving himself at the edge of the lawn! We quickly hustled him out of sight, back to his room and crossed all our fingers and toes that he'd sleep it off and be bright-eyed in time for his talk in 12 hours time. The next morning, our keynote speaker didn't turn up for the sound check. He was also a no-show at breakfast. There was no answer when we phoned his room. Eventually, five minutes before the symposium was due to begin, he finally responded to my colleague's insistent (read: frantic and slightly aggressive) hammering on the door to his hotel room. The speaker splashed some water on his face, put on a tie and appeared at the podium just in time to deliver what transpired to be a cogent, thoughtful and practical presentation, to rave reviews (although, by our assessment, it was noticeably wobbly in places). That year's event and keynote speaker received the highest ratings of any the client had ever sponsored.

Was this project a success? It certainly seemed so. Did it achieve its objectives? Yes, without question. But was it perfect? I think we all know the answer to that.

Perfection is not a reasonable measure for most professionals or assignments. PR is no exception here. There are many other more meaningful and appropriate standards that practitioners can hold themselves to, rather than aspiring to the holy grail of 'perfection'. I have listed 10 alternatives below as questions to ask oneself during the development of, and then throughout, any PR assignment or campaign. For me, these are worth striving for – far more so than perfection – and they truly define the success and value of our industry:

PLEASE NOTE: These are not to be confused with metrics for a specific assignment or campaign, which need to be developed on a case-by-case basis and evaluated using an array of analytics.

1. **Is my PR strategy aligned with business objectives?** How will what I am doing or proposing contribute to the reputation or perception of the company, organization or brand?

2. **Are my recommendations well-informed?** Specifically, have I considered the day-to-day lives of my stakeholders? Their point or points of view? What or who influences them? Do I know, based on this understanding, where we can find agreement between our company or brand's goals or aspirations and theirs?

3. **Can I support my recommendations with evidence?** Have I done my research? And, equally importantly, have I shown my data and cited credible sources? (When answering this question, Wikipedia should not be considered a citable source.)

4. **Have I delivered flawless documents?** Spelling and grammar-checking tools will not find every mistake. Never could. Never will. Your written output must be thoroughly edited: whether proposals, presentations, reports, content, press releases, tweets, captions, letters...*everything* needs to be proofread. Preferably by humans – at least two. Often, someone else will identify, with fresh eyes, an error you have repeatedly glossed over, despite multiple readings.

5. **Have I chosen the best channels for my target audience needs?** The breadth of options is broad and, honestly, exciting to everyone. The tools we use to amplify our messages can be game-changing for any strategy. Resist the urge to use the channels that you personally find interesting or useful; instead consider the routes that are most consumed and trusted by your stakeholders and are most appropriate for their particular audience and goals. This nuanced approach can make all the difference.

6. **Do my messages communicate with integrity?** Remember that we are not 'spinning' here. In every situation, it is vital that your message be trusted 100%.

7. **Do my PR recommendations integrate well with the other elements of the communications mix?** This is especially important in multichannel efforts and for campaigns at which PR is at the table with colleagues from Public Affairs, HR, Legal/Regulatory, advertising, marketing, or consulting firms (this is only a partial list). PR practitioners can and do partner with many other disciplines, and should forge productive and seamless working partnerships to ensure a cohesive message is delivered.

8. **Have I facilitated a two-way dialogue and/or created engagement?** Have I inspired? Have I found common ground with the stakeholders? Inserted something new, or changed the conversation about an issue or a brand? Have I made engaging with my brand, company, or organization easy to do?

9. **And, if you have created engagement, are you listening?** If you are listening, are you doing so in a sensitive and objective manner, acknowledging and/or including the differing points of view?

10. **And, finally, have I helped to create and/or enhance a relationship with my stakeholders?** Have I identified areas in which we agree? If there are any areas of disagreement or disconnection, what solutions have I provided to smooth these out?

CHAPTER 11

WHAT'S NEXT FOR PR?

*"Change is the law of life.
And those who look only to
the past or present are certain
to miss the future."*

John F. Kennedy[55]

Another perennial discussion within the industry is where is PR going and have we adequately prepared the next generation of practitioners to lead? A response I've frequently seen can be characterized like so: "The way forward is to go beyond PR" or "For PR to grow, we need to forge a different path". Both these mantras articulate that the core value of our function is currently insufficient for our changing times, and will become increasingly so in the future.

Paul Holmes, Chair of The Holmes Group, explains, "For me, what's happened to PR in the last 30 years is that it's become defined in relationship to other disciplines that are perceived as similar. PR is all too often defined by the use of earned media, when, in fact, there's nothing in PR that limits the tool kit or the channel, any one particular element of the mix or anything at all."

From a personal perspective, I believe that our skills as relationship builders using strategy, deep understanding of our audience and what positively influences them can take PR in an infinite number of directions, if we take care to develop both the art and the craft of our discipline. Communicating a point of view persuasively, amplifying it well, building trust that prompts an action, or changes behaviour, or creates community, or manages a crisis. It's all PR.

This is not to say that PR could or should do *everything*. PR is a complement to, but discernibly different from, marketing. Similarly, strategic PR is not strategic business consulting, though our disciplines work beautifully together to solve business issues. Moreover, while PR utilizes paid media more and more these days – it actually has done so since the 1950s – advertising agencies remain different, valuable and necessary.

My point here is simply that there is both the need and room for every discipline and we complement each other when we're at the table together. Although the tactics and channels we use may change, whether through technology or need, the fundamental business and practice of PR is broad and flexible and more important than ever.

"An analogy I use a lot is that PR practitioners used to be very concerned about our 'swim lane': Marketing was here, Human Resources was over there, Internal somewhere else and PR was somewhere between all of these. The big difference now is that PR is more like synchronized swimming. Sure, someone will sometimes get smacked in the face. But when it comes together well, it is a beautiful thing."

Kathryn Beiser, Chief Communications Officer and Senior Vice President, Kaiser Permanente

Growing as professionals is critical to growing our profession and ensuring it is relevant, needed and distinctive.

"Everyone needs to evolve, no matter what business you're in. This could mean growing your technical skill set or your leadership ability. Whether at the beginning, the middle or deep into their PR careers, practitioners need new experiences, partnerships with peers at other types of organizations, and exposure to people, assignments, discussions and situations that will allow them to become better, stronger PR professionals," maintains Dave Samson.

So, what does it mean to go 'beyond PR'? And is this type of alteration truly necessary for our continued growth? I think not.

PR is, can and should be here to stay. I believe our discipline does not have to evolve into something else in order to grow or be successful. Yes, we need to be observant, curious and agile, intelligent and empathetic, and always mindful of how to use communications to solve business needs. We won't have to fight to get a seat at the table and an appropriate share of attention or budget if we keep successfully delivering what we are trained to do.

A good message to leave you with is one Senator Elizabeth Warren has recently been credited with, though she is sure others have said it before her: "If you don't have a seat at the table, you're probably on the menu."[56] Warren was speaking to women when she used this quote, though it has the same powerful meaning here. PR needs practitioners strong in the art and the craft of our profession who help advance the discipline and its importance to the business of corporations and organizations now and for the future.

CHAPTER 12

MESSAGES FROM THE MASTERS

I have a journalist friend – a very serious and highly accomplished professional – who never takes new information at face value. He always requires multiple sources before either accepting a point of view or considering reporting on it. It is with his rigorous approach in mind that I want to provide readers with more than simply my perspective regarding our industry. So, for this final chapter, I asked a number of highly seasoned and sage PR professionals, many of whom are quoted throughout this book, what message they had for PR professionals working today and those considering entering this field. Even as a 30-year veteran of this business, I found their perspectives both inspiring and practical. I hope you will, too.

KATHRYN BEISER
CHIEF COMMUNICATIONS OFFICER
AND SENIOR VICE PRESIDENT,
KAISER PERMANENTE

It all starts with a strong, fundamental sense of business. You need to know the business objective of the company or issue you're supporting, how communications fits in to this, and to what end. You also need to understand *every* element of the business of the company or organization you're representing, whether it be a corporation, non-profit or an agency. This means you need a grasp of not only communications, but also of finance, marketing, employee relations, investor relations, government and policies – really the entire ecosystem of the space in which you're operating.

Besides business, you need to understand the forces that drive behaviour. You are operating in context. Always. If you don't get that, you don't get any further. You'll be operating in fragments.

As both a chief communications officer and agency executive, Kathryn Beiser has worked across a broad range of global industries during her career, including hospitality, consumer products, retail, financial services, healthcare and durable goods. She has held top-level positions including Executive Vice President of Corporate Communications for Hilton Worldwide, and Vice President of Corporate Communications for Discover Financial Services.

MICHAEL BLASH
GLOBAL HEAD OF INTERNAL COMMUNICATIONS,
MERCK

Michael Blash is an accomplished and enthusiastic senior-level corporate communications professional and business leader, with more than 20 years of experience in creating outstanding strategy, which translates into well-aligned execution.

There are three critical elements to being successful in PR that are enduring. Firstly, you need to be a killer writer. I don't care who you are, or what you do. If you are not a good writer, you are at a fundamental disadvantage. Killer writers don't start out that way. They hone their skills over time, with every chance they get.

Secondly, there is a great deal to be learned from the strategies and experiences of past practitioners: 1 year, 5 years, 10 years and even 50 years ago. Gain as much as you can from the past. As much as staying current is important, it is equally valuable to mine our discipline's history for lessons, case studies, and good models.

Finally, recognize bias. Your clients – whether you are working in an agency, on the corporate side or at a non-profit – need to be aware of, acknowledge and consider subjectivity accordingly. This is a part of communications integrity that can never be compromised.

NANCY CARAVETTA
JOINT CHIEF EXECUTIVE OFFICER, REBEL GAIL COMMUNICATIONS

You need to learn enough about every aspect of the ecosystem of the space you're working in. It is not necessary to be an expert, but a certain level of fluency in the issues and understanding of your stakeholders is absolutely required. This will enable you to give PR a credible voice and seat at the table. In terms of individual strengths, we all have strengths and weaknesses: areas where we prefer to work in preference to others; interests for which we have more passion than others. But I'd say it is not possible to be a successful PR practitioner unless you spend some time doing everything. At some point, you can become a specialist, but at all stages in your career – and not only at the beginning of it – you need to stay open.

Agencies need to give young people exposure to everything so they can see the whole picture – how one action or tactic impacts another.

Nancy Caravetta has worked at both large and small agencies throughout her career. A born entrepreneur, Nancy was the President and Founding Partner of the global healthcare boutique agency CPR Worldwide, following stints in several global agencies. Nancy has successfully launched more than 50 leading pharmaceutical products in the U.S. and across major markets around the world.

Finally, never forget that we're all human. Public relations is a human discipline and it is our responsibility to bring humanity to a company or organization's brand, message and actions. It is especially easy to lose this in the trend toward social, digital, mobile communications. These are just platforms. You need to be able to communicate a message *in person* in a room. You can't hide behind the platform. Strip all that away; if the message is not compelling, forget it. We're dealing with other humans. Find the way to connect – whether to your clients or to the brand or company's stakeholders.

People think that anyone can go into PR, but there's a particular type of personality who can be really successful at the whole discipline. It's what I tell my clients all the time – we're talking to human beings, one at a time. I remind them that they are not a company. A building. A product. A package. A logo. We're all human beings. We need to manage communications in human terms, and I ask them to ask themselves how they would want to be spoken to, how would they like to receive that piece of information; we must let that be our prevailing guide.

MARY LYNN CARVER
CHIEF COMMUNICATIONS OFFICER AND GLOBAL VICE PRESIDENT OF CORPORATE COMMUNICATIONS, GENERAL MILLS

Manage your career to gain a wide breadth of experiences; don't chase titles. I have a feeling Millennials will be better at this than we were. Be patient and recognize opportunities that align with your interests. Identify where you can contribute and make a difference, and seek out those projects. If you see a need and have the passion to do it, go for it – regardless of whether or not a promotion is involved.

Look beyond the rote part of your existing job. Remember that everybody's job, at every stage and level of responsibility, has a little mind-numbing stuff. The most efficient way to progress to more interesting work is to do the mundane aspects faster and better. Make sure you know why you're doing that three-times-daily media monitoring, or why the data analytics are important, or why that particular rote task is important to the overall assignment. Not only will mastering these basics make you better at doing them, you'll also learn a lot,

Mary Lynn Carver has served in senior level communications and public affairs positions in a variety of organizations, ranging from large multi-national companies such as AstraZeneca to high-tech start-ups. She also spent several years as the Chief Communications Officer for large non-profits, including the University of Maryland Medical System and St. Jude Children's Research Hospital. Mary Lynn is currently serving as the Global Chief Communications Officer of General Mills, home to household brands such as Cheerios, Annie's, Yoplait, Betty Crocker and Pillsbury.

if you let yourself. And you'll always learn even more if you know why the specific task is important.

Finally, when you're looking for your first couple of jobs, search for people you can learn from. Some of this may be related to the individual you'll be working for, while some may be linked to the environment you're working in.

EMILY DENNEY
VICE PRESIDENT, GLOBAL COMMUNICATIONS AND CORPORATE PHILANTHROPY, WEST PHARMACEUTICAL SERVICES, INC.

My advice for those getting into the PR field is to remember your important role of bringing the outside *in*. No one else within a company or organization is tasked with this role to a greater degree than those of us in PR, whether it's providing feedback on how the company is being perceived externally – positively or negatively; or if it involves forecasting how stakeholders might react to a potential action the company is considering; or even if it is a matter of sharing how employees are reacting, or will react, to an upcoming organizational announcement. The crucial factor is to maintain an awareness of the effect of the company's actions on the world beyond, and vice-versa. Your role as a PR professional is to ensure that leadership at your company (or your client) considers how any given message or action will land with the impacted stakeholders. It is only after a thorough evaluation of stakeholders' potential reaction to a message, activity or use of a specific channel that

Emily Denney is a skilled corporate affairs executive with 20 years of experience in senior roles in corporate communications, product public relations, financial media relations, issues/crisis management and external affairs. In her role as Vice President of Global Communications and Corporate Philanthropy for West Pharmaceutical Services, she is responsible for all external and internal global corporate communications and brand communications for the company, and manages West's corporate giving programmes.

companies can make a truly informed decision. When you consider the fact that bringing the outside in could change the course of how a company or organization acts, you can see just how important a PR role can be in an organization.

MIKE FERNANDEZ
CHIEF EXECUTIVE OFFICER,
BURSON-MARSTELLER

This has to be the most exciting time to think about a career in PR because of how integral communications not only is, but is also considered, in solving real world and business problems. It's not about communications in a vacuum.

George Bernard Shaw said: "The single biggest problem with communications is the illusion that it has taken place." In fact, it's not communications until it's understood. The point of that is it's not so much what we say or what we write that matters. Only when it is understood do you forge the kind of relationships that matter. That's what PR does: builds relationships, regardless of the medium.

So, I'd tell people considering PR as a profession, or those in the early stages of their careers: 1) Seek to understand others as much as you'd seek to be understood and 2) Approach any com-

Mike Fernandez has served as chief communications officer for five large U.S.-based corporations across diverse industries, including financial, technology, consumer goods and services, and health care. Most recently, he led global corporate affairs at Cargill, the world's largest privately held company and one of the world's leading producers and marketers of food, agricultural, financial and industrial products and services. He has been listed on *PRWeek*'s Power List and *The Holmes Report*'s Influence 100 list and was inducted into the *PRWeek* Hall of Fame in 2015.

munications challenge not as an exercise in communications but as a tool by which to solve problems.

PAUL HOLMES
PUBLISHER AND CHAIR, THE HOLMES GROUP

I would encourage all public relations practitioners today – not only those new or relatively new to this business – to think critically. If you can think with clarity, you can probably write with clarity. Those skills go hand in hand and they are what makes PR professionals so valuable. Challenging yourself to think in this way is an excellent reminder, both to yourself and to your clients, that you are offering so much more than craft. If you aspire to be the best type of PR professional, you need a combination of learnable skills, which can be taught and grown with practice, and personal character traits. These have to come from inside as well as through exposure to good mentors.

Courage is one example. You need to be willing to stand up in a room of people who need to find a solution and say, if you really believe this is true, that the only real solution is the hardest one; not the quick or simple fix. Curiosity and empathy are

Paul Holmes, Publisher and Chair of The Holmes Group, has been writing about public relations for more than 25 years. Early in 2000, Paul launched The Holmes Group, which provides knowledge and insight to public relations professionals across a variety of platforms. The group's flagship title, *The Holmes Report*, covers the public relations business in the Americas, Europe, the Middle East and Africa and the Asia-Pacific region. In 2011, Paul was inducted into the ICCO Hall of Fame.

other character traits that PR counsellors and practitioners need. I cannot overstate the importance of integrity, without which there is no credibility. By integrity, I'm talking about real intellectual honesty.

Finally, in today's world – and likely tomorrow's – agility is a must. You need to be able to respond in real time to new challenges and new information because the speed of shit happening is just incredible. I'd advise everyone in this business to spend as much time developing these traits as possible: at least as much time as they invest in developing infographics, videos, social media and the other tools.

JON IWATA
FORMER SENIOR VICE PRESIDENT AND
CHIEF BRAND OFFICER, IBM

Never underestimate the importance of mastering the timeless fundamentals. Those, together with an acute sense of timing, understanding what message and when that message is needed, are enduring communications skills, now and in the future. There is a very clear and distinct set of skills that make PR professionals and their contributions unique to the organization they are supporting. Among the most important values we bring is our ability to articulate what sets the client/company/institution apart and then ensuring that internal stakeholders understand these distinctions, embrace them, and behave accordingly.

While public relations is an excellent vehicle for communicating a company's ethics, the practice of public relations should not be confused with 'ethics' themselves.

Consider how companies like Nike and Apple communicate. These are companies widely admired for communicating their

Jon served as Chief Brand Officer at IBM and the architect of the company's strategic brand platforms, including e-business, Smarter Planet and Watson. He is recognized for innovation – from creating Think Academy, an online university serving more than 380,000 IBMers, to the application of cognitive technologies in marketing and communications. Jon is recognized as a leader in both the marketing and corporate communications professions. He is an inductee of the Marketing Hall of Fame, the CMO Club Hall of Fame and the Page Society Hall of Fame.

uniqueness to internal and external stake-holders – everybody understands what these companies believe, what they stand for.

We have the sensibility, the tools and the words to help companies think through their distinctive position in not only their space but in the world.

My final message to young PR practitioners is to recognize from a business perspective what the trend of highly personalized, one-on-one communications means. This is a shift from stakeholder segmentation. Technology and data allow companies to engage people as individuals but also at scale. Realizing the opportunities for communications as a result are ahead of us.

MARGERY KRAUS
FOUNDER AND EXECUTIVE CHAIRMAN, APCO WORLDWIDE

The next generation of public relations professionals needs to be worldly in their outlook and understand their role in the contract between business and society.

They should see themselves as custodians for their company's values and aim high. They're on the front lines.

Communications is not a passive exercise – it's not just about one brand or a set of messages or activities and the need to promote. It's as much about shaping these things from the start; the act of sitting at the table: blowing the whistle when the messaging or the actions are inconsistent with the values.

Diversity of backgrounds and perspectives, together with empathy are musts. I don't know how it is possible to effectively represent an organization, or understand and then communicate its place in society, if the leadership team and communications

Margery Kraus, Founder and Executive Chairman of APCO Worldwide, a global consulting firm headquartered in Washington, D.C., specializes in public affairs, communication and business consulting for major multinationals. Margery's' achievements have been recognized by a number of prestigious awards, including the *PRWeek* Hall of Femme (2017); PR News' PR People Hall of Fame (2015); C200 Foundation Entrepreneurial Champion Award (2015); *PRWeek* Hall of Fame (2014) among others.

partners all come from the same place. Understanding your stakeholders' perspectives – their emotional drivers as well as their business positions – is key. You can't do that without a deep dive into their day-to-day lives, both through data analytics and also experientially. What good is it to be diverse if you're not inclusive?

We need to teach the next generation of PR professional the skills of being persuasive without being offensive and it seems, in the current political environment, that there are a lot of these nuances we are unlearning right now. As we go forward, we need to teach our next generation of practitioners that there is a non-confrontational way to convey a point of view, which resonates with others, but you need to really *listen* to them first to be successful.

STEVE LAMPERT
FORMER EXECUTIVE DIRECTOR OF PUBLIC AFFAIRS, ASTRAZENECA

Always remember you are part of a team. This requires you to understand all the functions of a company including its business and its goals, as well as all the roles and responsibilities of your colleagues. You need to understand what they do, how they work, and what they need to be successful. This information is necessary for you to make yourself and your communications skills invaluable. You need to be flexible – adaptability is key.

Steve Lampert spent 23 years at AstraZeneca leading the Brand Corporate Affairs department, where he was responsible for product communications strategy. He also served on the Corporate Affairs Leadership Team responsible for global and corporate strategies. He is currently a full service public affairs and communications advisor.

Today's business environment is global and instantaneous. Social media makes this a 24/7 communications world. Cast a wide net in terms of the media you follow, not only for a specific assignment or the sources you personally follow.

Caution has always been critical but it seems to be more so now. By 'caution' I am not referring to political correctness. That's another important issue. But here, I want to underscore the need to think things through from every perspective. Scenario planning needs to be thorough.

Stay informed as a human being. Be connected, not only to the space you're operating in on a professional basis, but also in terms of world business, politics, sports and pop culture. Read all points of view. This approach will only make you a better communicator.

KELLY MCGINNIS
SENIOR VICE PRESIDENT AND CHIEF
COMMUNICATIONS OFFICER,
LEVI STRAUSS & CO.

I think PR is inextricably linked to a broader social conscience. I tell my team that a significant part of our role at Levi Strauss is to serve as our company's social conscience – and with this positioning comes significant responsibility. How a company communicates is more important now than it's ever been. It's exciting.

I'd offer two pieces of advice. The first is not exclusive to PR careers. Listen to yourself. Be self-aware. Recognize when you're making decisions out of fear – whether it is a fear of change, or a fear of taking on something you don't know how to do – take a deep breath and realize those are exactly the things that you should tackle head on and overcome. Looking back, you'll wonder why it took you so long to do so.

Secondly, and this one is specific to PR: take seriously our role as the 'conscience of our organizations'. It's our job to bring the voices of our stakeholders to the table

Kelly McGinnis has been the Chief Communications Officer and Senior Vice President of Corporate Affairs at Levi Strauss & Co. since August 2013. Kelly oversees a global team that includes media relations, internal communications, government affairs, consumer relations, community affairs and the LS&Co. archives. She has over 20 years of experience as a senior communications leader.

and ensure their perspectives are understood and considered in our organizations.
That means engaging with the press, protecting the enterprise by advocating for
integrity and empathy in every interaction
and communication that we touch.

CHARLOTTE OTTO
FORMER GLOBAL EXTERNAL RELATIONS
OFFICER, PROCTER & GAMBLE

This is an exciting time for public relations. The arenas in which we apply our skills are unlimited. There is no issue that doesn't have a communications or public policy aspect to it. Similarly, the arenas that benefit from strategic communications leadership are limitless.

We need to stay true to what specifically differentiates public relations professionals from other disciplines and that means developing well-honed expertise and skills. Otherwise, there is a danger in becoming a 'generalist' and not bringing unique value to the business. In fact, I think we need to bring an *irreplaceable* set of skills: we need to demonstrate an understanding of the communications implications of a changing external environment, from politics to the business dynamic and the media, and who is influencing them and what kind of engagement we need to have. It's important that we understand the implications for the company then, with regard to messaging

Ms. Charlotte R. Otto served as Global External Relations Officer of Procter & Gamble Co for 33 years, gaining experience and overseeing assignments in Beauty and Family Care, New Products, and Public Affairs. Charlotte is a Member of the Arthur Page Society, Chair of Downtown Cincinnati Inc. and of the Cincinnati Playhouse in the Park, Vice-Chair of the Greater Cincinnati Chamber of Commerce and a member of the Port of Greater Cincinnati Development Authority.

and programming. We interpret all of these influences and make them actionable for a brand or a company. These are critical elements of business problem solving and equal in value to the output of strategic business consultants.

My suggestion for the next generation of practitioners is to learn how business runs; this will make your contributions to the table more valuable. For the deepest experience here, I'd even recommend going out and running a business – not as a communicator but as someone talking to customers and responsible for delivering value and accountable to your peers, your customers, your investors. This will give you the truest sense of business and the role of communications. Seek those opportunities.

JULIANNA RICHTER
CHIEF OPERATING OFFICER, EDELMAN U.S.

This is the most exciting time to be in our industry because it's essential for us to be the kind of partner that companies need. Our understanding of what it takes to build, protect and evolve reputations and relationships – together with our knowledge of the latest communications channels – give us the license to deliver effective solutions. The flip side of this is that the industry is also the most complex it has ever been, especially once you overlay the changes in the world and the new technologies available. PR has always helped keep companies on their front foot; this is what makes us more valuable now than ever. I'd emphasize to new practitioners, and also to emerging leaders in our industry, the importance of staying current. It's a challenge and this requires us to be mindful of how we spend our time (both personally and professionally) but we can be a force for positive change and can deliver the best and most impactful thinking to our clients.

Julianna Richter is the U.S. Chief Operating Officer of Edelman, Inc. and previously served as President of Global Client Relationship Management.

DAVE SAMSON
GENERAL MANAGER OF PUBLIC AFFAIRS, CHEVRON

Dave Samson is General Manager of Public Affairs for Chevron Corporation, a position he has held since 2004. His team is responsible for Chevron's communications strategies and activities, including digital/social engagement, media relations, employee engagement, executive communications, issues management and litigation communications. Dave's team is also responsible for corporate branding, advertising, research and analytics.

In our business, what we have to offer is experience and integrity. So my advice is to seize new experiences to show your clients, if you're on the agency side. In a corporate setting, it is important for executive leaders to be shown what integrity looks like, sounds like, reads like; ultimately what communicating integrity means to and for that company. And remind them to never compromise on this.

In terms of personal development, always remain curious. Never stop growing. Every year, you need to give up 20% of what you already do well and take on 20% of something new, something you don't know. A mentor of mine told me that. And given the rapid evolution of our industry and what's happening today, it is more important than ever to keep evolving yourself. And it has to be by design, and on your own terms, or the change will be forced upon you.

Finally, don't take yourself too seriously. Have fun. Keep everything in perspective.

HELEN C. SHELTON
SENIOR PARTNER, FINN PARTNERS

As my mother still tells me to this day, "When you get a seat at the table, you'd better bring more than your appetite."

Seek inspiration everywhere. Pursue excellence in everything. There is no shortcut in communications. Constantly think of things both from a strategic and from a creative perspective, in order to remain fresh so that you have something to add.

Find out ways we can work in an integrated space and be careful not to compartmentalize – either yourself or the discipline.

Helen Shelton is a Senior Partner at global communications agency, Finn Partners Inc. She is a communications strategist specializing in the development and implementation of national and international public relations programmes for Fortune 500 companies, as well as non-profit cultural and social service organizations. Named one of the 25 Most Influential Black Women in Business by *The Network Journal* magazine, Helen recently received the Circle Award for Excellence in Communications from ColorComm.

ELLIOT SLOANE
SENIOR MANAGING DIRECTOR, FTI CONSULTING

Elliot Sloane is a Founder of Sloane & Company LLC and served as its Chief Executive Officer. He managed integrated financial communications programmes for AT&T, Gaylord Entertainment, TiVo, American Express, the Bermuda International Business Association, New York Life, Cablevision and Boone Pickens, among others. He is the recipient of two Silver Anvil Awards in investor relations for work performed on behalf of BellSouth Corporation and the Flight International Group.

When I was first starting out in PR, I met with industry executives I admired and I asked them if it was possible to make a million dollars a year in PR. I posited that it was not. They set me straight, and I distinctly remember one of them saying, "Yes you can. You do it by being invaluable." That response has always stuck with me.

If you want to build not only a meaningful career, but one in which you are compensated at the level equal to that of other senior advisors, you need to deliver something significant, tangible and measurable. To me, that means giving clients smart, thoughtful advice they can't get from anybody else and a practical plan: something ambitious but absolutely achievable.

Not only should you aim to be smart, but you should also aspire to be fast thinking, clear-eyed and straight talking. Your stakeholders should not only respect you, but also fall a little in love with you.

There's a bit of seduction at play, too.

You have to want to be the best and keep working at it. You need to wake up every day and believe you're going to be the best in the world at what you do. Mediocrity is not acceptable. PR is work – sometimes it's hard work – and when you're starting out, you need to pay your dues. Work your ass off. You need to be all in. Not just ankle-deep. It doesn't mean that you're not going to flounder and scramble: you will. But effort really counts.

Build a network of influencers in a really strategic way. Everybody moves around and they will remember you. Meet those people early; cultivate positive relation-ships and one day these people will become referral sources.

FRANKLIN WALTON PH.D.
STRATEGIC COMMUNICATIONS CONSULTANT

Dr. Walton is principal of Franklin Walton LLC. For more than 30 years, he held various roles including Chief Knowledge Officer and Performance Officer at several Ruder Finn companies. Frank holds a Ph.D. in Communications Theory and English Literature from the University of Illinois at Urbana-Champaign.

I stress to PR students, and to those beginning their careers, the importance of taking the broad view of our practice in order to develop the perspective and way of thinking that is intrinsic to considered, effective and truly strategic PR. This means understanding business, sociology, politics and behavioural psychology. It is helpful but not necessary to 'study' PR, per se. The background you get from a degree in history, philosophy, political science, journalism and psychology can all lead to a successful career in PR. I always think of a former colleague of mine who has a Ph.D. in Italian Literature from Harvard and an MBA from Cass Business School in London; these are traditionally the 'wrong' qualifications, but have actually proved to be exactly the 'right' qualifications to form an exemplary public relations professional.

You also need to cultivate a deep knowledge of the business and industry sector you're in. This is more important than your tactical skills – whether these be digital or social. You need keen ability, real strengths at the tactical end, but you should always be thinking in terms of the big picture.

RESOURCES

ORGANIZATIONS:

- Public Relations Society of America and local chapters of PRSA
  https://www.prsa.org/

- The Arthur Page Society
  http://www.awpagesociety.com/

- The Institute for Public Relations
  http://www.instituteforpr.org/

- Museum of Public Relations:
  http://www.prmuseum.org/

READING MATERIAL:

In addition to staying current on world news, market news, industry news and pop culture, I recommend the following outlets become part of your regular rotation:

- *PRWeek*
  http://www.prweek.com/us

- *The Holmes Report*
  https://www.holmesreport.com/

- *AdAge*: Particularly the CMO Strategy
  http://adage.com/section/cmo-strategy-columns/481

- *The Harvard Business Review*, both the magazine
  and the blog

- Carol Kinsey Goman, Ph.D. is an international
  keynote speaker and author of The Silent Language
  of Leaders: How Body Language Can Help
  – or Hurt – How You Lead and The Truth
  About Lies in the Workplace.

- *AP Style Guide* or *The Chicago Guide*

- Encounter Program and Resilient Listening
  http://www.encounterprogrammes.org/wp-content/
  uploads/2012/07/FINAL.-Introduction-to-
  Encounters-Comm-Agreement.May15.12.pdf

- *Make Your Bed* by Admiral William H. Mcraven
  https://www.amazon.com/Make-Your-Bed-Little-
  Things/dp/1455570249

- Bill Gates' message to 2017 graduates
  https://mic.com/articles/176935/bill-gates-has-a-
  message-for-every-college-grad-who-wants-to-
  change-the-world#.84Qc1htod

- Bill Gates' commencement message to 2017 graduates
  https://www.gatesnotes.com/About-Bill-Gates/
  Dear-Class-of-2017

- About T. Boone Pickens
  http://www.boonepickens.com/

- Susan Fowler, *Motivating People Doesn't Work and What Does: The New Science of Leading, Energizing and Engaging*

- Steven Covey, *The 7 Habits of Highly Effective People: Powerful Lessons in Personal Change*

VIEWING MATERIAL:

- Eminem interview
  https://www.youtube.com/watch?v=4hr0Q-x-QNM
  https://www.youtube.com/watch?v=lPcR5RVXHMg

- 2017 Commencement Address at Harvard given by Mark Zuckerberg
  https://www.youtube.com/watch?v=BmYv8XGl-YU

- 2005 Steve Jobs' Commencement Address at Stanford
  https://www.youtube.com/watch?v=D1R-jKKp3NA

- 2014 Commencement Address at the University of Texas at Austin given by Admiral William H. McRaven
  https://www.youtube.com/watch?v=pxBQLFLei70

- Eminem on '60 Minutes' with Anderson Cooper and rhymes with orange
  https://www.youtube.com/watch?v=_kQBVneC30o

AWARDS:

PR case studies of award-winning programmes are accessible. There are many very worthy programmes; I have provided only a short list below.

- Silver Anvil
  http://apps.prsa.org/awards/silveranvil/#.
  WXDQx9Pyv-Y

- SABRE
  https://www.holmesreport.com/events-awards/
  sabre-awards

- PRWeek
  http://www.prweek.com/us/awards

- Cannes Lions PR Awards
  https://www.canneslions.com/awards/the-lions/pr

- Bulldog Reporter awards
  https://www.bulldogreporter.com/awards/

- The ONE Club
  http://www.oneclub.org/

FAILURES:

I also recommend searching for, and learning about, the PR efforts that have proved *un*successful because these are also hugely instructive. Not surprisingly, these are not archived in any one, neat place. Scour the internet. Talk to people; any seasoned PR executive will have a story to tell.

EPILOGUE:
A FINAL WORD

Often returning to the roots is the best way to go forward.

Practitioners of PR will benefit from the pioneering work and thinking that make our profession valuable, business-critical and a must-have. This focus on the *art* of PR seems an imperative now, at a time when the emphasis on new tools, exciting channels and new media is so dominant. Successful campaigns should be built on their ability to connect people to each other, to companies, to brands or an issue. They should build positive relationships and communicate meaningfully. While the latest whiz-bang tactics may have a role, even a central role in the execution, the ideas themselves should not be valued simply for their novelty.

I also wanted to encourage students of philosophy, psychology, human behaviour and other social sciences to feel they have a path into PR. And, conversely, for journalism, PR and media students to expose themselves to a wider range of classes, such as business and business management. The industry needs all of these skills in order to thrive and continue providing perspective and distinct worth. By approaching work with a holistic view and true integrity, it is possible to build a rich and thriving company, able to weather the fast-paced changes of today's world.

Finally, there are numerous resources available that go far deeper into many of the subjects I've touched upon in this book. I have listed a few of these in the Resources section. The opportunities to read, hear, learn, and experience more to improve your abilities as a PR practitioner are practically limitless. I hope you will see the Notes and Further Reading section and be inspired to read more widely and study more wisely. Many sage and seasoned professionals who gave so much of their time in interviews with me have written articles and books, rich in experience, vision and direction. They also speak at industry events. I encourage you to seek them out and be open to learn from the wealth of wisdom they and others have to offer.

NOTES AND FURTHER READING

NOTES TO CHAPTER 1

1. Bernays, Edward L. "Father of Public Relations' And Leader in Opinion Making, Dies at 103." New York Times (1995). Accessed November 11, 2017. http://www.nytimes.com/books/98/08/16/specials/bernays-obit.html?mcubz=3

2. Van Camp, Scott. "2012 PR News Hall of Fame: David Finn." PR News (2012). Accessed November 11, 2017. http://www.prnewsonline.com/2012-pr-news-hall-of-fame-david-finn/

3. The Museum of Public Relations. *n.d.* Accessed October 10, 2017. http://www.prmuseum.org/

4. Landman, Anne. "BP's 'Beyond Petroleum' campaign losing its sheen." PR Watch (2010). Accessed November 11, 2017. https://www.prwatch.org/news/2010/05/9038/bps-beyond-petroleum-campaign-losing-its-sheen

5. Grunig, J.E., and Todd Hunt. *Managing Public Relations.* Austin, TX: Holt, Rinehart and Winston, 1984.

6. Morris, Trevor. "Are Grunig and Hunt still relevant?" PRWeek (2014). Accessed November 11, 2017. http://www.prweek.com/article/1291832/grunig-hunt-relevant

7. Turney, Michael. "Asymmetric v. symmetric public relations." NKU (1998). Accessed November 11, 2017. https://www.nku.edu/~turney/prclass/readings/3eras3x.html

Further reading:
Bernays, Edward L. *Biography of an Idea: Memoirs of Public Relations Counsel Edward L. Bernays.* New York: Simon and Schuster, 1965

Bernays, Edward L. (Swift, Paul, ed.). *The Later Years: Public Relations Insights 1956-1986.* Rhinebeck, NY: H&M Publishers, 1986

NOTES TO CHAPTER 2

8. Popova, Maria. "Chuck Close on creativity, work ethic, and problem-solving vs. problem-creating." Brainpickings (2012). Accessed November 11, 2017. https://www.brainpickings.org/2012/12/27/chuck-close-on-creativity/

9. Shpigel, Ben. "With rigor and mystique, Nebraska builds a bowling dynasty." New York Times (2017). Accessed November 11, 2017. https://www.nytimes.com/2017/04/11/sports/nebraska-bowling-lady-cornhuskers.html

10. Einstein, Albert. *n.d.* Accessed October 10, 2017. https://www.goodreads.com/quotes/7718768-once-you-stop-learning-you-start-dying

11. The Pursuit of Happiness. "Martin Seligman Psychology." Accessed November 11, 2017. http://www.pursuit-of-happiness.org/history-of-happiness/martin-seligman-psychology/

12. Deloitte Consulting LLP. "Transitioning to the future of work and the workplace." Accessed November 11, 2017. https://www2.deloitte.com/content/dam/Deloitte/global/Documents/HumanCapital/gx-hc-us-cons-transitioning-to-the-future-of-work-and-the-workplace.pdf

13. Sandifer, Carly. "Anton Chekhov's six writing principles." OneWildWord.com (2011). Accessed November 11, 2017. https://onewildword.com/2011/11/14/anton-chekhov%E2%80%99s-six-writing-principles

14. Dweck, Carol S. *Mindset: The New Psychology of Success.* New York, NY: Random House, 2006.

NOTES TO CHAPTER 3
15. Dyer, Wayne W. "Success secrets." Accessed November 11, 2017. http://www.drwaynedyer.com/blog/success-secrets/

NOTES TO CHAPTER 4
16. Einstein, Albert. *n.d.* Accessed October 10, 2017, https://www.brainyquote.com/quotes/quotes/a/alberteins121643.html

17. Brooks, David. "The creative monopoly."
    New York Times (2011). Accessed November 11, 2017.
    http://www.nytimes.com/2012/04/24/opinion/
    brooks-the-creative-monopoly.html.

18. Liesse, Julie. "What clients want."
    OMD 10th Anniversary: That Was Then,
    This Is Now (2012): c6. Accessed November 11, 2017.
    http://brandedcontent.adage.com/pdf/OMD10_
    anniversary.pdf

19. Zuckerberg, Mark. "Commencement address
    at Harvard." Harvard Gazette (2017). Accessed
    November 11, 2017. https://news.harvard.edu/gazette/
    story/2017/05/mark-zuckerbergs-speech-as-written-for-
    harvards-class-of-2017/

20. Richards, Carl. "Want to be creative on purpose?
    Schedule it." New York Times, (2017). Accessed
    November 11, 2017. https://www.nytimes.
    com/2017/05/15/your-money/want-to-be-creative-on-
    purpose-schedule-it.html.

21. Tesla, Nikola. n.d. Accessed November 11, 2017.
    https://www.goodreads.com/quotes/962527-be-alone-
    that-is-the-secret-of-invention-be-alone.

22. Leonhardt, David. "You're too busy. You need
    a 'Schultz hour.'" New York Times (2017).
    Accessed November 11, 2017. https://www.nytimes.
    com/2017/04/18/opinion/youre-too-busy-you-need-a-
    shultz-hour.html.

NOTES TO CHAPTER 5

23. Covey, Stephen R. *n.d.* Accessed October 10, 2017. https://www.goodreads.com/quotes/298301-most-people-do-not-listen-with-the-intent-to-understand

24. Goman, Carol Kinsey. "3 crucial skills for leading without authority." Forbes (2017). Accessed November 11, 2017. https://www.forbes.com/sites/carolkinseygoman/2017/05/21/3-crucial-skills-for-leading-without-authority/#76a2f6a54a80

25. Zeno of Citium. *n.d.* Accessed October 10, 2017. https://www.goodreads.com/author/quotes/833825.Zeno_of_Citium

26. Seppala, Emma, and Jennifer Stevenson. "In a difficult conversation, listen more than you talk." Harvard Business Review (2017). Accessed November 11, 2017. https://hbr.org/2017/02/in-a-difficult-conversation-listen-more-than-you-talk

27. Oster, Erik. "Marketers plan to increase PR spending over the next 5 years, according to new report." Adweek (2017). Accessed November 11, 2017. http://www.adweek.com/agencies/marketers-plan-to-increase-pr-spending-over-the-next-5-years-according-to-new-report/

28. Encounter Communication Guidelines. Accessed November 11, 2017. http://www.encounterprograms.org/wp-content/uploads/2012/07/FINAL.-Introduction-to-Encounters-Comm-Agreement.May15.12.pdf

29. Alan Alda in conversation with Neil deGrasse Tyson. "What does it mean to be a true communicator?" Accessed October 10, 2017. https://www.facebook.com/92ndstreetY/videos/10154988234193884/?fref=mentions

NOTES TO CHAPTER 6

30. Sartre, Jean-Paul. *n.d.* Accessed October 10, 2017. https://www.goodreads.com/quotes/6300-words-are-loaded-pistols

31. Eminem interview with Anderson Cooper on *60 Minutes*. Accessed July 23, 2017. https://www.youtube.com/watch?v=4hr0Q-x-QNM and https://www.youtube.com/watch?v=_kQBVneC30o

32. Scrabble®. Accessed October 10, 2017. https://scrabble.hasbro.com/en-us

33. Bananagrams®. Accessed October 10, 2017. http://www.bananagrams.com/

NOTES TO CHAPTER 7

34. Angelou, Maya. *n.d.* Accessed October 10, 2017. https://www.goodreads.com/quotes/5934-i-ve-learned-that-people-will-forget-what-you-said-people

35. McRaven, William H. Commencement address at the University of Texas at Austin on May 17, 2014. Accessed November 11, 2017. https://www.youtube.com/watch?v=pxBQLFLei70.

36. McRaven, William H. *Make Your Bed: Little Things That Can Change Your Life...and Maybe the World.* New York, NY: Grand Central Publishing, 2017.

37. Jobs, Steve. Commencement addressat Stanford University on June 12, 2005. Accessed October 10, 2017. https://www.youtube.com/watch?v=D1R-jKKp3NA

38. Zuckerberg, Mark. Commencement address at Harvard University on Mary 25, 2017. Accessed October 10, 2017. https://www.youtube.com/watch?v=BmYv8XGl-YU

39. Gates, Bill. "Dear class of 2017..." Accessed May 15, 2017. https://www.gatesnotes.com/About-Bill-Gates/Dear-Class-of-2017

40. Pinker, Steven. *The Better Angels of Our Nature.* New York, NY: Viking, 2011.

41. Fowler, Susan. *Motivating People Doesn't Work and What Does: The New Science of Leading, Energizing, and Engaging.* San Francisco, CA: Berrett-Koehler Publishers, 2014.

42. Zak, Paul J. "The neuroscience of trust," Harvard Business Review (2017). Accessed October 10, 2017. https://hbr.org/2017/01/the-neuroscience-of-trust

43. Gandhi, Mahatma. *n.d.* Accessed October 10, 2017. http://www.quotationspage.com/quote/36464.html

NOTES TO CHAPTER 8

44. Edison, Thomas Alva. *n.d.* Accessed October 10, 2017. https://www.brainyquote.com/quotes/quotes/t/thomasaed125942.html.

45. Oster, Erik. "How agencies are shifting strategies to compete with Accenture and Deloitte." AdWeek (2017). Accessed November 11, 2017. http://www.adweek.com/brand-marketing/how-agencies-are-shifting-strategies-compete-accenture-and-deloitte-175401/

46. Schultz, EJ. *n.d.* "The race is on!" AdAge. Accessed November 11, 2017. http://adage.com/article/news/consultancies-rising/308845/

47. Shaw, George Bernard. 1921 (in *Back to Methuselah*). Accessed October 10, 2017. https://www.brainyquote.com/quotes/quotes/g/georgebern162023.html

48. Thaler, Richard H. *Misbehaving, The Making of Behavioral Economics.* New York: W.W. Norton & Company, Inc. 2015

NOTES TO CHAPTER 9

49. *The Godfather*, 1972 (Paramount Home Video, 1999). Accessed October 10, 2017. https://www.youtube.com/watch?v=0qvpcfYFHcw

50. Temin, Davia. "How United Became the World's Most Hated Airline in One Day." Forbes (2017). Accessed November 11, 2017. https://www.forbes.com/sites/daviatemin/2017/04/11/how-united-became-the-worlds-most-hated-airline-in-one-day/#10b721ac61f2.

51. Harris Poll. "United Airlines' corporate reputation takes a nose dive." *The Harris Poll* (2017). Accessed November 11, 2017. http://www.theharrispoll.com/business/United-Airlines-Reputation-Nose-Dive.html.

52. Nadella, Satya. "Satya Nadella email to employees as first day as CEO." Microsoft News Center (2014). Accessed November 11, 2017. https://news.microsoft.com/2014/02/04/satya-nadella-email-to-employees-on-first-day-as-ceo/

NOTES TO CHAPTER 10

53. Voltaire. *n.d.* Accessed November 11, 2017. https://www.goodreads.com/quotes/search?utf8=%E2%9C%93&q=Voltaire%2C+perfect&commit=Search

54. Beard, Alison. "Life's work: an interview with Alan Alda. Harvard Business Review (2017). Accessed November 11, 2017. https://hbr.org/2017/07/alan-alda.

NOTES TO CHAPTER 11

55. John F. Kennedy. *n.d.* Accessed November 2017. https://www.brainyquote.com/authors/john_f_kennedy

56. Elizabeth Warren. *n.d.* Accessed November 2017. https://www.brainyquote.com/quotes/elizabeth_warren_690853

ACKNOWLEDGMENTS

I am deeply indebted to many people, who have inspired me professionally and personally over the years. Among them:

Kirk Stewart, the ultimate connector, and one of the most insightful communications leaders and partners I have had the privilege of knowing, and, more recently, working with.

All the accomplished, admired and respected leaders in the industry who gave their valuable time and thoughts to this project (listed alphabetically): Kathy Beiser, Michael Blash, Nancy Caravetta, Mary Lynn Carver, Emily Denney, Mike Fernandez, Paul Holmes, Jon Iwata, Margery Kraus, Steve Lampert, Kelly McGinnis, Charlotte Otto, Julianna Richter, Dave Samson, Helen Shelton, Elliot Sloane and Frank Walton.

Mandy O'Donnell, for reading through my draft with the her sharp eye, and providing the kind of informed feedback that only comes with 25 years of PR experience, knowledge and insight plus a generous dose of love.

Frank Walton, who invited me to teach in the newly created Brand & Integrated Communications (BIC) master's degree programme at City College of New York, where my father went to college and where I am on faculty. Frank is among the most thoughtful, insightful and kindest people I've ever met in the public relations business. He's also the best dressed.

Nancy R. Tag, ever-inspiring Director of BIC. Also, BIC faculty colleague Frank Washkuch, News Editor at *PRWeek*, who edited and published the article of mine that made me think I had a book.

The writers whose work I admire, and writers I am lucky enough to know, whose ability and fluency to communicate, whether facts or fiction, leaves me in awe. Rich Turner, former Editor at the *Wall Street Journal* who embodies everything trustworthy and reliable about journalism, and Adam Snyder, are just two of the most awesome.

The many clients, peers and colleagues I've had throughout my career.

Students in my classes, workshops and boot camp sessions. The Roman philosopher Seneca said, "While we teach, we learn." This has been true for me.

Vivian Fisher, who, for more than 11 years, has been by my side every morning pounding the trails of Central Park and we still have plenty to talk about.

Rae and Irwin Stahl, my parents, who instilled in me the values and perspective that have governed every step I've taken.

Jeremy Jacob, my husband and partner in life, parenting and business, whose love and unfailing, boundless and selfless support has surprised and humbled me for over 30 years.

Our children, Sophie, Jesse and Jack, who challenge me every day to think more deeply, choose my words more carefully, have more patience, try harder, laugh more and strive to be an all-around better version of the person and mother I was the day before.

© Karen Smul

AN INTRODUCTION TO
SANDRA STAHL

Sandra is a recognized thought leader in public relations strategy and audience connectivity. She has authored articles for *AdAge*, *PRWeek*, *PM360*, *Pharmaceutical Executive*, *Fox News* outlets, *WomenEntrepreneur* and the *Journal of the American Dental Association*, among others.

In her agency and corporate positions, and as co-founder of jacobstahl since 2003, Sandra has shaped communications strategies and campaigns for companies of all sizes, from leading multinationals to start-ups, as well as non-profit organizations and academic institutions.

Sandra is considered especially valuable to her clients and colleagues for the creativity and stakeholder insights she brings to communications solutions and her ability to distil the complex into the manageable. She has extensive experience in brand, corporate and internal communications with a distinctive strength in developing narratives that contribute to relationships that matter.

Sandra is on faculty at the Brand & Integrated Communications graduate program at the City College of New York. She lives in New York and is married with three children.

25TH
LID
ANNIVERSARY

Sharing knowledge since 1993

- 1993 Madrid
- 2008 Mexico DF and Monterrey
- 2010 London
- 2011 New York and Buenos Aires
- 2012 Bogotá
- 2014 Shanghai